CONTENTS

KU-526-394

This PHRASE BOOK is thematically colour-coded for easy use and is organized according to the situation you're most likely to be in when you need it. The fairly comprehensive DICTIONARY section consists of two parts – English/French and French/English.

To make speaking French easy, we encourage our readers to memorize some general PRONUNCIATION rules (*see* page 8). After you have familiarized yourself with the basic tools of the language and the rudiments of French GRAMMAR (*see* page 14), all you need to do is turn to the appropriate section of the phrase book and find the words you need to make yourself understood. If the selection is not exactly what you're looking for, consult the dictionary for other options.

Just to get you started, here are some French expressions you might have heard, read or used at some time: *réservoir, pièce de résistance, déjà-vu, hors-d'œuvre, lingerie*. Even if you are unfamiliar with these words and would rather not try to say them out loud, just remain confident, follow our easy advice and practise a little, and you will soon master useful phrases for everyday life. Speak slowly and enunciate carefully and your counterpart is likely to follow suit.

Some French words, especially those ending in -ion, are pronounced differently from their English equivalents (e.g. Situation – *see twah syon*), or else changed just slightly (politician – *politicien*), though their meanings remain clear. Nowadays many English terms are used in French, especially in business, sport and leisure activities, so everyone will know what you mean when you say things like 'laptop', 'golf' and 'tennis'.

A section on HOLIDAYS AND FESTIVALS (*see* page 82) provides some background knowledge so that you know what you're celebrating and why. There's no better way to learn a language than joining in some enjoyment!

The brief section on manners, mannerisms and ETIQUETTE (*see* page 76) can help you make sense of the people around you. Make the effort to view your host country and its people tolerantly – that way you will be open to the new experience and able to enjoy it.

5

Learning a new language can be a wonderful but frightening experience. It is not the object of this book to teach you perfect French, but rather to equip you with just enough knowledge for a successful holiday or business trip. Luckily you are unlikely to be criticized on your grammatical correctness when merely asking for directions. The most important thing is to make yourself understood. To this end a brief section on grammar and a guide to pronunciation have been included in this book. There is, however, no substitute for listening to native speakers.

Before you leave, it might be a good idea to familiarize yourself with the sections on Pronunciation, Grammar and Etiquette. This can easily be done en route to your destination. You will also benefit from memorizing a few important phrases before you go.

The sections of the Phrase Book are arranged by topic for quick reference. Simply go to the contents list (*see* page 3) to find the topic you need. The Dictionary section (*see* page 88) goes both ways, helping you to understand and be understood.

Abbreviations have been used in those instances where one English word could be interpreted as more than one part of speech, e.g. 'smoke' (a noun, the substance coming from a fire) and 'smoke' (a verb, what one would do with a cigarette). Here is a list of these and some other abbreviations used in this book:

vb	verb
n	noun
adj	adjective
adv	adverb
pol	polite
fam	familiar (informal)
elec	electric/al
med	medical
anat	anatomy
rel	religion

The gender and number of French nouns have been specified as follows:

m	masculine
f	feminine
pl	plural

French has strong vocalic characteristics, so vowels must be clearly sounded.

VOWELS
VOYELLES

◆ **a**	like the **a** in cat
◆ **e**	like the **u** in but
	(given as **uh** in this book)
◆ **é**	like the **a** in late
◆ **è, ê**	like the **e** in ten
◆ **i**	like the **ee** in see
◆ **o**	like the **o** in or
◆ **u**	like the **u** in Susan
	(given as **ew** in this book)
◆ **au, eau, ô**	like the letter **o**
◆ **e, eu**	like the **ur** in hurt
◆ **ou**	like the **oo** in cool

NB The letter **e** without an accent is not sounded when it appears at the end of a word.

NASAL SOUNDS
NASALES

◆ **an, am, en, em**	like the **an** in answer
◆ **in, im, ain, ein, un**	like the **uh** in uh-huh
◆ **on, om**	like **song** without the g

SEMI-VOWELS
SEMI-VOYELLES

- **ill**　　　　　　　like the **y** in yet
- **ui**　　　　　　　like the **wee** in sweet
- **oi**　　　　　　　like the **oi** in reservoir

CONSONANTS
CONSONNES

- **c before i or e**　　like the **s** in sit
- **ç before a, o, u**　like the **s** in sit
- **ch**　　　　　　　like the **sh** in shoe
- **gn**　　　　　　　like the **ni** in onion
　　　　　　　　　　(given as **ñ** in this book)
- **g before e or i**　　like the **g** in beige
　　　　　　　　　　(given as **zh** in this book)
- **j**　　　　　　　　like the **g** in beige
　　　　　　　　　　(given as **zh** in this book)
- **qu**　　　　　　　like the **k** in kiss

THE LETTER S
LA LETTRE S

- **s at the beginning of a word** – like the **s** in sit
- **ss between two vowels** – like the **s** in sit
- **s between a consonant and a vowel** – like the **s** in sit
- **s between two vowels** – like the **z** in zoo

MORE CONSONANTS
AUTRES CONSONNES

- **r** is pronounced at the back of the tongue.
- **h** at the beginning of a word is never sounded, so 'hôtel' is pronounced 'ôtel'.

NB As a general rule a consonant at the end of a word is never sounded. There are only a few exceptions, mainly with monosyllabic or short words, like *cher*, *sac*, *donc*, *hiver*, *avec*, etc, where the last consonant is pronounced.

LIAISON
LIAISON

This is a situation when the last consonant of a word links up with the first vowel of the following word:

- 'Comment allez-vous?' (How are you?) is πpronounced '*comman-tallay-voo*?'
- 'ils ont' (they have) is pronounced 'il zont'

French does not have strongly stressed syllables, and we have not indicated stress points. Native speakers do place a slight stress on the last syllable of a word, but there are numerous exceptions and regional variations.

PRONUNCIATION

Practise these phrases to get the hang of it!

Bonjour!
bonzhoor
Good day

Au revoir!
or revwaah
Good bye

Parlez-vous anglais?
parlay-voo onglay
Do you speak English?

Je ne comprends pas
zhuhn conpronpah
I don't understand

Parlez plus lentement
parlay plew lontmong
Speak more slowly

Comment ça va?
common sah vah
How are you? (Familiar)

Comment allez-vous?
commontallay-voo
How are you? (Polite)

Très bien, merci!
tray byah, mairsee
Very well, thank you

Pardon
pardong
Pardon me

Merci!
mairsee
Thank you

S'il vous plaît
sill voo play
Please

quatre, sept, huit
katr, set, weet
four, seven, eight

Est-ce que je peux ...?
esker zhuh puh
Can/may I ...?

Je voudrais ...
zhuh voodray
I would like ...

Hier
eeair
Yesterday

Aujourd'hui
ohzhoordwee
Today

Demain
demung
Tomorrow

Où sont les toilettes ?
ooh saw lay twahlet
Where are the toilets?

Il y a ...
Ill ee yah
There is/are ...

Qui est-ce?
kee e ser
Who is it?

C'est ...
say
It is ...

à gauche, à droite
a goash, a drwat
on the left, on the right

deux heures moins le quart
durze ur mwan luh car
quarter to two

le vingt-et-un juin
luh vant ay an jwan
the twenty-first of June

The grammar section has deliberately been kept very brief as this is not a language course.

NOUNS
NOMS

French nouns can have one of two genders (masculine or feminine), reflected in the article:

- **le/un garçon (m)** – the/a boy
- **la/une fille (f)** – the/a girl
- **le/un livre (m)** – the/a book
- **la/une maison (f)** – the/a house

To form the plural, an **s** must be added to both the masculine and the feminine words, but it is never sounded:

- **les garçons** – the boys
- **les filles** – the girls
- **les livres** – the books
- **les maisons** – the houses

ADJECTIVES
ADJECTIFS

Adjectives will follow the same rule and be masculine or feminine depending on whether they qualify a masculine or feminine word.

With most adjectives, the feminine form is achieved simply by adding an **e** to the masculine form:

- **intelligent** (m) – clever
- **intelligente** (f) – clever

NB In the masculine form, the last consonant (in the example above the **t** of 'intelligent') is not sounded, but on the other hand the consonant is sounded in the feminine form – 'intelligente' is pronounced *intelligent*.

When it comes to the plural form, adjectives again follow the same rule as nouns, adding an **s** (which is not sounded) for the plural:

- **des garçons intelligents** – clever boys
- **des filles intelligentes** – clever girls

In French, most adjectives follow the nouns they qualify rather than preceding them as in English. There are, however, exceptions to this rule, for example *petit/petite* (small), *grand/grande* (large), and a few others which are mostly monosyllabic and very commonly used adjectives, like *beau* (beautiful) and *bon* (good). These precede the nouns they qualify.

VERBS
VERBES

PRESENT TENSE (PRÉSENT)

Verbs are conjugated according to three main patterns, indicated by the ending of their infinitive forms:

- All verbs ending in **-er**, like **arriver** (to arrive)
- Most verbs ending in **-ir**, like **finir** (to finish)
- Most verbs ending in **-dre**, like **attendre** (to wait for)

A fourth group comprises all verbs that do not belong to any of the above groups. They have an irregular conjugation. Among these are the auxilliary verbs.

AUXILIARY VERBS (VERBES AUXILIARES)

The 'vous' form, apart from being the plural for 'tu', is used to address in the singular form people other than family and friends.

For all verbs, regular or irregular, the main forms to know are those corresponding to 'I' (je) and 'you' (vous):

- ◆ **j'arrive** – I arrive
- ◆ **vous arrivez** – you arrive
- ◆ **je finis** – I finish
- ◆ **vous finissez** – you finish
- ◆ **j'attends** – I wait for
- ◆ **vous attendez** – you wait for

SOME IRREGULAR VERBS (VERBES IRRÉGULIERS)

can	**je peux** – I can
	vous pouvez – you can
want	**je veux** – I want
	vous voulez – you want
do/make	**je fais** – I do/make
	vous faites – you do/make
go	**je vais** – I go
	vous allez – you go
take	**je prends** – I take
	vous prenez – you take
leave	**je pars** – I leave
	vous partez – you leave

PAST TENSE (PASSÉ)

Form the past tense with the auxiliaries **avoir** or **être** plus a **past participle**. The past participles of the three main groups are:

- verbs ending in -er: **é** (arriver – **arrivé**)
- verbs ending in -ir: **i** (finir – **fini**)
- most verbs ending in -dre: **du** (attendre – **attendu**)

Most verbs take **avoir** as an auxiliary:
- **j'ai attendu** – I waited
- **vous avez fini** – you finished

Some verbs describing a transfer from A to B take **être** as an auxiliary:
- **je suis arrivé** – I arrived
- **vous êtes parti** – you left

Here are some examples of a few more verbs conjugated with **être**:
- **aller** – to go:
  je suis allé – I went
- **venir** – to come:
  je suis venu – I came
- **descendre** – to come down:
  je suis descendu – I came down
- **monter** – to go up:
  je suis monté – I went up

NEGATIVE FORM (NÉGATIF)

For the **present** tense, the negative is obtained by adding **ne** in front of the **verb**, and **pas** after:

- je **ne** veux **pas**; je **n'**ai **pas**; vous **ne** partez **pas**

For the **past** tense, the negative is obtained by adding **ne** in front of the **auxiliary verb**, and **pas** after it:

- je **n'**ai **pas** attendu – I did not wait
- je **ne** suis **pas** parti – I did not leave

INTERROGATIVE FORM (INTERROGATIF)

The most common form of turning a sentence into a question is to add the expression '**est-ce que**' (pronounced *eske*) in front of the verb:

- **est-ce que vous comprenez?** – do you understand?
- **est-ce qu'il est arrivé?** – did he arrive/has he arrived?

However, a few verbs are commonly used in another form:

- **pouvez-vous?** – can you?
- **avez-vous?** – do you have?

Useful Question Forms (Questions Utiles)

- **est-ce qu'il y a ...?** – is/are there ...?
- **qu'est-ce que ...?** – what do/does ...?
- **quand est-ce que ...?** – when do/does ...?
- **où est-ce que ...?** – where do/does ...?
- **pourquoi est-ce que ...?** – why do/does ...?

ARTICLES
ARTICLES

The article in French is used as follows:

Definite Article (Article Défini) – the

le (masc. sing.)   *la* (fem. sing.)

les (masc. pl.)   *les* (fem. pl.)

Examples:

le chien (the dog)   *la plage* (the beach)

les chiens (the dogs)   *les plages* (the beaches)

Indefinite Article (Article Indéfini) – a, some

un (masc. sing.)   *une* (fem. sing.)

des (masc. pl.)   *des* (fem. pl.)

Examples:

un chien (a dog)

une plage (a beach)

des chiens (some dogs)

des plages (some beaches)

NUMBERS
NOMBRES

0	zéro	*(zayroh)*
1	un	*(ung)*
2	deux	*(duh)*
3	trois	*(trwah)*
4	quatre	*(kahtr)*
5	cinq	*(sunk)*
6	six	*(seess)*
7	sept	*(set)*
8	huit	*(weet)*
9	neuf	*(nuhf)*
10	dix	*(deess)*
11	onze	*(onz)*
12	douze	*(dooz)*
13	treize	*(trays)*
14	quatorze	*(kahtorz)*
15	quinze	*(kunz)*
16	seize	*(sayz)*
17	dix-sept	*(deesset)*
18	dix-huit	*(deezweet)*
19	dix-neuf	*(deeznuhf)*
20	vingt	*(vung)*
21	vingt et un	*(vung tay ung)*
22	vingt-deux	*(vungt-duh)*
30	trente	*(tront)*
40	quarante	*(karont)*
50	cinquante	*(sunkont)*
60	soixante	*(swahssont)*
70	soixante-dix	*(swahssont-deess)*

71	soixante et onze	*(swahssontay onz)*
72	soixante-douze	*(swahsoont-dooz)*
73	soixante-treize	*(swahsoont-trays)*
74	soixante-quatorze	*(swahsoont-kahtorz)*
75	soixante-quinze	*(swahsoont-kunz)*
76	soixante-seize	*(swahsoont-sayz)*
77	soixante-dix-sept	*(swahsoont-deesset)*
78	soixante-dix-huit	*(swahsoont-deezweet)*
79	soixante-dix-neuf	*(swahsoont-deeznuhf)*
80	quatre-vingts	*(katruh-vung)*
90	quatre-vingt-dix	*(katruh-vung-deess)*
100	cent	*(song)*
101	cent-un	*(song-ung)*
120	cent-vingt	*(song-vung)*
1000	mille	*(meel)*
1 million	un million	*(ung meelyong)*
1 billion	un milliard	*(ung meelyahr)*

MONTHS
MOIS

January
janvier *(zhonvyay)*

February
février *(fairvreeyay)*

March
mars *(mars)*

April
avril *(aavreel)*

May
mai *(may)*

June
juin *(zhwa)*

July
juillet *(zhweeyay)*

August
août *(ooh)*

September
septembre *(septonbr)*

October
octobre *(octobr)*

November
novembre *(novonbr)*

December
décembre *(desonbr)*

DAYS
JOURS

Monday
lundi *(lundee)*

Tuesday
mardi *(mardee)*

Wednesday
mercredi *(maircredee)*

Thursday
jeudi *(zhuhrdee)*

Friday
vendredi *(vondredee)*

Saturday
samedi *(samdee)*

Sunday
dimanche *(deemonsh)*

weekdays
jours de la semaine, jours
ouvrables *(zhoor duh la
smain, zhoor oovraab)*

in three days
dans trois jours
(dong trwa zhoor)

TIME AND DATE
HEURE ET DATE

in the morning
le matin *(luh maatung)*

in the afternoon
l'après-midi
(lahpray meedee)

in the evening
le soir *(luh swaar)*

What is the time?
Quelle heure est-il?
(Kelerr aytill)

It's ...
Il est ... *(Illay...)*

- **quarter past two**
- deux heures et quart
  (duhzerraycar)

- **twenty past two**
- deux heures vingt
  (duhzerr vung)

- **half past two**
- deux heures et demie
  (duhzerraydmee)

- **quarter to three**
- trois heures moins
  le quart
  (trwazerr mwunlcar)

- **midnight**
- minuit *(meenew-ee)*

- **early**
- tôt *(toe)*

- **late**
- tard *(tar)*

at 10 a.m. (10:00)
à dix heures *(ah deeserr)*

at 5 p.m. (17:00)
à dix-sept heures
(ah deesseterr)

today
aujourd'hui
(orzhoordwee)

day after tomorrow
après demain
(ahpraidmung)

day before yesterday
avant hier *(ahvontyair)*

this morning
ce matin *(suh mahtung)*

yesterday evening
hier soir *(eeyair swahr)*

tomorrow morning
demain matin
(duhmung mahtung)

25

tomorrow
demain *(duhmung)*

yesterday
hier *(eeyair)*

last night
la nuit dernière
(lah nwee dernyair)

this week
cette semaine
(set sirmen)

next week
la semaine prochaine
(lah sirmen proshain)

now
maintenant *(muntnah)*

after lunch
après le déjeuner
(ahpray luh dayzhuhnay)

soon
bientôt *(byahtoe)*

What is today's date?
Quel jour sommes-nous aujourd'hui? *(Kel zhoor somnoo orzhoordwee)*

It's 20 December
Le 20 décembre *(Luh vung daysombre)*

GREETINGS
SALUTATIONS

Good morning/ afternoon
Bonjour *(Bonzhoor)*

Good evening
Bonsoir *(Bonswaar)*

Good night
Bonne nuit *(Bonnwee)*

Hello
Salut *(Salew)*

Goodbye
Au revoir *(Ohrvwaar)*

Cheerio
Salut, ciao
(Salew, tchahoh)

See you soon
À bientôt *(Ah byahtoe)*

See you later
À plus tard *(Ah plew tar)*

Have a good trip
Bon voyage
(Bon vwahyazh)

Have good time
Amusez-vous bien
(Ahmewsay voo byah)

I have to go now
Il faut que je file
(Illfoh kuh zhuh fill)

My name is ...
Je m'appelle ...
(Zhuh mahpail)

What is your name?
Quel est votre nom?
(Kelay votruh nong)

May I intoduce ...
Je vous présente ...
(Zhuh voo praysont)

Pleased to meet you
Enchanté(e) *(Onshontay)*

How are you?
Comment allez-vous?
(pol) *(Commaantallayvoo)*
Comment ça va? (fam)
(Commaansah vah)

Fine. And you?
Très bien, merci. Et vous?
(pol) *(Tray byah, mairsee.
Ay voo)*
Bien, merci, et toi? (fam)
(Byah, mairsee. Ay twah)

Isn't it a lovely day?
Quelle belle journée!
(Kel belzhoornay)

Just a minute!
Un instant! *(Ununstong)*

GENERAL
GÉNÉRALITÉS

Do you speak English?
Parlez-vous anglais?
(Parlay voo onglay)

I don't understand
Je ne comprends pas
(Zhuhn congprong pah)

Please speak very slowly
Parlez très lentement
s'il vous plaît *(Parlay plew
lontmong sillvooplay)*

Please repeat that
Pouvez-vous répéter
(Poovay voo raypaytay)

Please write it down
Pouvez-vous écrire ça,
s'il vous plaît *(Poovay voo
aycreer sah, sillvooplay)*

Excuse me please
Excusez-moi
(Ayxcewzay mwah)

Could you please help me?
Pouvez-vous m'aider, s'il
vous plaît? *(Poovay voo
mayday sillvooplay)*

BASICS

how?
comment? *(commaan)*

where?
où? *(oo)*

when?
quand? *(kong)*

who?
qui? *(kee)*

why?
pourquoi? *(poohrkwah)*

which?
quel(le)? *(kel)*

I need ...
J'ai besoin de ...
(Zhay buhzwa duh)

please
s'il vous plaît *(sillvooplay)*

thank you
merci *(mairsee)*

yes
oui *(we)*

no
non *(nong)*

Sorry!
Pardon! *(Pahrdong)*

FORMS & SIGNS
FORMULAIRES
& SIGNALISATIONS

**Please complete
in block letters**
À remplir en lettres
majuscules
*(Ah rompleerong
mazhuhscewl)*

Surname
Nom *(Nong)*

First names
Prénoms *(Praynong)*

Date of birth
Date de naissance
(Daht duh nayssonss)

Place of birth
Lieu de naissance
(Lyuh duh nayssons)

Occupation
Profession *(Profayssyong)*

Nationality
Nationalité *(Nasionaleetay)*

Address
Adresse *(Adress)*

Passport number
Numéro de passeport
(Nuhmayrow duh passpor)

I.D. number
Numéro de carte
d'identité *(Numayrow
de cart deedonteetay)*

Issued at
Délivré à *(Dayleevray ah)*

Date of arrival
Date d'arrivée
(Dat darreevay)

Date of departure
Date de départ
(Dat duh daypar)

Engaged, Vacant
Occupé, Libre
(Ocewpay, Leebr)

No trespassing
Propriété privée
(Propreeyaytay preevay)

Sold out
Épuisé *(Aypwe-eezay)*

Out of order
En panne *(Ong pun)*

Please don't disturb
Prière de ne pas
déranger *(Preeyair duh
neh pah dayronzhay)*

Office hours
Horaire des bureaux
(Orrair day bewhroh)

Push, Pull
Poussez, Tirez
(Poohsay, Teeray)

Lift/Elevator
Ascenseur *(Assonsserr)*

Escalator
Escalier roulant
(Airscahlyay roolon)

**Ground Floor, First
Floor, Top Floor**
Rez-de-chaussée,
Premier Étage, Dernier
Étage *(Raydshorsay,
Pruhmyay raytahzh,
Dayrnyai raytahzh)*

Wet paint
Peinture fraîche
(Puntewr fraysh)

Open, Closed
Ouvert, Fermé
(Oovair, Fairmay)

Till/Cash Desk
Caisse *(Caiss)*

Adults and children
Adultes et enfants
(Ahdewltay onfon)

Closed on Mondays
Fermé le lundi
(Fairmay leh lundee)

BUS/TRAM STOP
ARRÊT DE
BUS/TRAMWAYS

Where is the bus station/tram stop?
Où est l'arrêt d'autobus/du tram? *(Ooay lahray dohtohbews/dew trung)*

Which bus do I take?
Je dois prendre quel bus? *(Zhuh dwah prondr kel bews)*

How often do the buses go?
Il y a un bus tous les combien? *(Illyah ung bews too lay kombyah)*

When is the last bus?
Quelle est l'heure du dernier bus? *(Kel ay lerr duh dernyay bews)*

Do I have to change?
Est-ce que je dois changer? *(Esker zhuh dwah shonzhay)*

What is the fare to ...?
Combien coûte le trajet pour ...? *(Kombyah coot luh trahzhay)*

I want to go to ...
Je veux aller à ... *(Zhuh wuh allay ah ...)*

Which ticket must I buy?
Je dois acheter quel ticket? *(Zhuh dwah ashtay kel teekay)*

Can you give me change?
Avez-vous la monnaie? *(Avay voo lah monnay)*

Where must I go?
Je dois aller où? *(Zhuh dwah allay oo)*

UNDERGROUND/ SUBWAY/METRO
MÉTRO

entrance
entrée *(ontray)*

exit
sortie *(sortee)*

Where is the underground station?
Où est la station de métro? *(Oo ay lah stahsiong duh metro)*

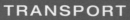

inner zone, outer zone
lignes internes, périphérie
*(leeñ untairn,
payreefairee)*

**RER (high-speed
train across Paris)**
Réseau express régional
(air uh air)

**Do you have a map
for the metro?**
Avez-vous un plan du
métro? *(Avay voo ung
plon duh metro)*

I want to go to ...
Je veux aller à ...
(Huh vuh allay ah ...)

**Can you give me
change?**
Avez-vous la monnaie?
(Avay-voo lah monnay)

**When is the next
train?**
Quand passe la
prochaine rame? *(Kon
pus lah proshayn rum)*

**How long will it be
delayed?**
Combien de temps va
durer le délai? *(Kombyah
duh tong vah dewray luh
duhlay)*

TRAIN/RAILWAY
TRAIN/SNCF

**Where is the railway
station?**
Où est la gare?
(Oo ay lah gahr)

departure
départ *(daypahr)*

arrival
arrivée *(ahreevay)*

Which platform?
Quel quai? *(Kel kay)*

A ticket to ... please
Un billet pour ... s'il
vous plaît *(Ung beeyay
poohr ... sillvooplay)*

◆ **single ticket**
◆ un aller simple
   (unallay sumpl)

◆ **return ticket**
◆ un aller-retour
   (unallay-ruhtoor)

◆ **a child's ticket**
◆ un billet tarif enfant
   *(ung beeyay
   tahreefonfon)*

- **first class**
- première classe
  (pruhmyair class)

- **second class**
- seconde classe
  (segond class)

- **non-smoking**
- non-fumeur
  (nong fewmuhr)

Do I have to pay a supplement?
Est-ce qu'il y a un supplément à payer?
(Eskillyah ung sewplaymong ahh payay)

Is my pass valid on this train?
Est-ce que ma carte d'abonnement est valide pour ce train? *(Esker mah cart dahbonmong ay vahleed pohr suh trung)*

Where do I get off?
Je dois descendre où?
(Zhu dwah daysondroo)

Do you have a timetable?
Vous avez un indicateur des horaires? *(Voozavay ununndeecahtuhr dayzohrair)*

I want to book ...
Je voudrais réserver ...
(Zhuh voodrayraysairvay)

- **a seat**
- une place *(ewn plahs)*

- **a couchette**
- une couchette
  (ewn cooshet)

Is this seat free?
Cette place est libre?
(Set plahs ay leebr)

That is my seat
C'est ma place
(Say mah plahs)

May I open/close the window?
Je peux ouvrir/fermer la fenêtre? *(Zhuh puh oovreer/fairmay lah fuhnaitr)*

Where is the restaurant car?
Où est le wagon-restaurant? *(Oo ay luh vahgong restohrong)*

Is there a sleeper?
Est-ce qu'il y a un wagon-lit? *(Eskillyah ung vagong-lee)*

TGV (high-speed train)
Train à Grande Vitesse

SNCF (French Railways)
Société Nationale des Chemins de Fer Français

information
renseignements *(ronsayñuhmong)*

platform indicator
indicateur des quais *(undeecatuhr day kay)*

left luggage lockers
consigne *(conseeñ)*

What station is this?
C'est quel arrêt/quelle gare? *(Say kelahray/ kel gahr)*

BOATS
NAVIGATION

cruise
croisière *(crwazyair)*

When is the next boat?
Quand est le prochain départ? *(Kong ay luh proshung daypahr)*

Can we hire a boat?
Peut-on louer un bateau? *(Puhtong lway ung bahtoe)*

How much is a round trip?
Combien coûte un aller-retour? *(Kombyah coot unallay-ruhtoor)*

Can we eat on board?
Peut-on déjeuner à bord? *(Puhtong dayzhuhnay ahbohr)*

When is the last boat?
Quand passe le dernier bateau? *(Kong pus luh dairnyay bahtoe)*

When is the next ferry?
Quand passe le prochain ferry-boat? *(Kong pus luh proshayn fairee-boht)*

How long does the crossing take?
Combien dure la traversée? *(Kombyah dewr lah trahvairsay)*

Is the sea rough?
Est-ce que la mer est houleuse? *(Esker lah mair ay ooluhz)*

TAXI
TAXI

Please order me a taxi
Pouvez-vous m'appeler un taxi *(Poovay-voo mahplay ung taxi)*

Where can I get a taxi?
Où est-ce que je peux prendre un taxi? *(Oo esker zhuh puh prondr ung taxi)*

To this address, please
A cette adresse, s'il vous plaît *(Ah setaddress, sillvooplay)*

To the airport, please
A l'aéroport, s'il vous plaît *(Ahlahayrohpor, sillvooplay)*

To the station, please
A la gare, s'il vous plaît *(Ah lah gahr, sillvooplay)*

To this hotel, please
A cet hôtel, s'il vous plaît *(Ah setohtel, sillvooplay)*

How much will it cost?
Combien coûtera la course? *(Kombyah cootrah lah coors)*

How long will it take?
Ça prendra combien de temps? *(Sah prondrah kombyah duh tong)*

I have nothing smaller
Je n'ai pas de monaie *(Zhuh nay pah duh monnay)*

Keep the change
Gardez la monnaie *(Garday lah monnay)*

I need a receipt
Je voudrais un reçu *(Zhuh voodray ung ruhsew)*

AIRPORT
AÉROPORT

arrival
arrivées *(areevay)*

departure
départs *(daypahr)*

domestic flights
vols intérieurs *(voluntayryuhr)*

flight number
numéro de vol *(newmayroh duh vol)*

gate
porte *(port)*

check-in
enregistrement/check-in
(onruhzheestruhmong/ checkin)

Where do I check in for ...?
Où est l'enregistrement pour ...? *(Oo ay lon-ruhgeestruhmong poohr)*

hand luggage
bagage à main
(bahgahzhahmung)

boarding card
carte d'embarquement
(cartuh donbarkuhmong)

last call
dernier appel
(dairnyairahpail)

valid, invalid
valide, non valide
(vahleed, nonvahleed)

baggage claim
livraison des bagages
(leevraysong day bahgazh)

luggage trolley
chariot *(shahryoh)*

lost property office
objets trouvés
(obzhay troovay)

Where do I get a bus to the centre?
Où est-ce qu'il y a un bus pour le centre-ville? *(Oo eskillyah ung bews poohr luh sontruh veel)*

An aisle/window seat, please
Un couloir/une fenêtre, s'il vous plaît
(ung coolwahr/ewn fuhnaytr sillvooplay)

customs
douane *(dwahn)*

I have nothing to declare
Rien à déclarer
(Ryahnah dayclahray)

Do I have to pay duty on this?
Est-ce que je dois payer une taxe pour ça? *(Esker zhuh dwah payay ewn tax poohr sah)*

The flight has been cancelled/delayed
Le vol est annulé/a été retardé *(Luh vol aytahnewlay/ah aytay ruhtarday)*

ROAD TRAVEL/
CAR HIRE
VOITURE/LOCATION

Have you got a map?
Vous avez une carte routière? *(Voozavay ewn cart rootyair)*

Which is the best route to ...?
Quel est la meilleure route pour ...? *(Kelay lah mayerr root poohr ...)*

Where is the nearest garage?
Où est le garage le plus proche? *(Oo ay luh garazh luh plew prosh)*

Fill it up, please
Faites le plein, s'il vous plaît *(Fet luh plung, sillvooplay)*

Please check the oil, water, battery, tyres
Pouvez-vous vérifier l'huile, l'eau, la batterie, les pneus *(Poovay-voo vayreefyay lweel, loh, lah bahtree, lay pnuh)*

I'd like to hire a car
Je voudrais louer une voiture *(Zhuh voodray lway ewn vwahtewr)*

How much does it cost per day/week?
Quel est le prix à la journée/semaine? *(Kelay luh pree ah lah zhoornay/smain)*

What do you charge per kilometre?
C'est combien au kilomètre? *(Say combyah oh kilometr)*

Is mileage unlimited?
Est-ce que le kilométrage est illimité? *(Esker luh kilo-metrazh ayt illeemeetay)*

What documents do I need?
Quels papiers me faut-il? *(Kel pahpyay muh fohtill)*

Where can I pick up/leave the car?
Où est-ce que je peux prendre livraison de/déposer la voiture? *(Oo esker zhuh puh prondr leevrayzong duh/daypohsay lah vwahtewr)*

motorway/freeway
autoroute *(autoroot)*

traffic report
état de la circulation *(aytah duh lah sirkewlahsyong)*

headlight
phare *(fahrr)*

engine
moteur *(mohtuhr)*

windscreen
Pare-brise *(pahr-breez)*

4x4 vehicle
quatre-quatre
(caht-cahtr)

What is the speed limit?
Quelle est la vitesse limite? *(Kelay lah veetess leemeet)*

The engine is overheating
Le moteur est surchauffé *(Luh mohtuhr ay sewrshhfay)*

Have you got ...?
Est-ce que vous avez ...? *(esker voozavay ...)*

♦ **a towing rope**
♦ un câble de remorque *(ung cahbl duh ruhmok)*

♦ **a spanner**
♦ une clé anglaise *(ewn clay onglayz)*

♦ **a screwdriver**
♦ un tourne-vis *(ung toornuh vees)*

The keys are locked in the car
Les clés sont enfermées dans la voiture *(Lay clay sontonfairmay dong lah vwahtewr)*

SIGNS
PANNEAUX
INDICATEURS

No through road
Impasse *(Unpus)*

one-way street
sens unique *(sonsewneek)*

entrance, exit
entrée, sortie *(ontray, sortee)*

Keep the entrance clear
Ne pas gêner l'accès de l'entrée *(Nuh pah zhaynay laksay duh lontray)*

Residents only
Réservé aux locataires *(raysayrvay oh lohcatair)*

pedestrians
piétons *(pyaytong)*

38

danger
danger *(dongzhay)*

speed limit
limitation de vitesse
*(leemeetahsyong duh
veetess)*

stop
stop *(stop)*

roundabout
détour *(daytoor)*

Insert coins
Introduisez des pièces de
monnaie *(Untrohdweezay
day pyays duh monnay)*

No parking
Défense de stationner
(dayfons duh stahsyonay)

parking garage
parking *(parking)*

supervised car park
parking gardé
(parking gahrday)

No right turn
Défense de tourner
à droite *(Dayfons duh
toornay ah drwat)*

cul-de-sac
impasse/cul-de-sac
(unpus/cewdsac)

roadworks
travaux *(trahvoh)*

basement
sous-sol *(soosol)*

detour
détour *(daytoor)*

**No admission for
unauthorised persons**
Interdit aux personnes
non autorisées
*(Untairdee oh pairson
non ohtohreezay)*

Caution
Attention *(Ahtonsyong)*

No admittance
Défense d'entrée
(Dayfons dontray)

No stopping
Stationnement interdit
*(Stahsyonmong
untairdee)*

No overtaking
Défense de doubler
(Dayfons duh dooblay)

Cycle path
Piste cyclable
(Peestuh seeclabl)

Toll
Péage *(Pay-azh)*

ACCOMMODATION
LOGEMENT

hotel
hôtel *(ohtel)*

bed & breakfast
chambre d'hôte
(shombruh doht)

vacancies
chambres libres
(shombruh leebr)

Have you a room ...?
Avez-vous une chambre
libre ...? *(Ahvay-voo ewn
shombruh leebr ...)*

◆ **for tonight**
◆ pour cette nuit
(poohr set nwee)

◆ **with breakfast**
◆ avec petit-déjeuner
*(ahvayk puyhee
dayzhuhnay)*

◆ **with bath**
◆ avec salle de bains
(ahvayk sal duh bung)

◆ **with shower**
◆ avec douche
(ahvayk doosh)

◆ **a single room**
◆ pour une personne
(poohr ewn paison)

◆ **a double room**
◆ pour deux personnes
(poorh duh pairson)

◆ **a family room**
◆ pour une famille
(poohr ewn fahmeey)

**How much is the
room per day/week?**
Quel est le prix de la
chambre par jour/à la
semaine? *(Kelay luh pree
duh lah shombr pahr
zhoor/ah lah suhmain)*

**Have you anything
cheaper/better?**
Vous n'avez rien de
moins cher/de mieux?
*(Voo navay ryah duh
mwung shair/duh myuh)*

**I want a room on
the ground floor**
Je voudrais une chambre
au rez-de-chaussée
*(Zhuh voodray ewn
shombr oh raydshohssay)*

room service
service en chambre
(sairvees ong shombr)

41

Do you have a cot?
Avez-vous un berceau?
(avay-voo ung bairsoh)

Do you have a high chair?
Avez-vous une chaise de bébé? *(Ahvay-voo ewn shaiz duh baybay)*

Please bring ...
Pouvez-vous apporter ...
(poovay-voo ahportay ...)

♦ **toilet paper**
♦ du papier hygiénique
(duh papyay eezhyayneek)

♦ **soap**
♦ du savon *(duh sahvong)*

♦ **clean towels**
♦ des serviettes propres
(day sairvvyet propr)

Please clean ...
S'il vous plaît, faites le ménage de ... *(Sillvooplay, fet luh maynazh duh ...)*

♦ **my room**
♦ ma chambre
(mah shombr)

♦ **the bath**
♦ la salle de bains
(lah sal duh bung)

Please put fresh sheets on the bed
Pouvez-vous changer les draps du lit
(Poovay-voo shonzhay lay drah dew lee)

Please don't touch ...
S'il vous plaît, ne touchez pas à ... *(Sillvooplay nuh tooshay pah ah ...)*

♦ **my briefcase**
♦ mon porte-document
(mong portuh-dohcewmong)

♦ **my laptop**
♦ mon ordinateur
(mon ordeenahterr)

♦ **my suitcase**
♦ ma valise *(mah valeez)*

Please come back later
Pouvez-vous revenir plus tard *(Poovay-voo ruhvuhneer plew tar)*

My toilet doesn't work
Les toilettes sont en panne *(Lay twahlet sontonpan)*

There's no hot water
Il n'y a pas d'eau chaude
(illnyah pah doh showd)

42

Are there any messages for me?
Est-ce qu'il y a des messages pour moi?
(Eskillyah day mayssazh poohr mwah)

My key, please
Je peux avoir ma clé *(Zhuh puh ahvwahr mah clay)*

Where is the lift?
Où est l'ascenseur?
(Oo ay lahsongserr)

Is there a laundry service?
Est-ce qu'il y a un service blanchisserie?
(Eskillyah ung sairvees blonsheesree)

What number do I dial for room service?
Quel numéro dois-je appeler pour le service d'étage? *(Kel newmay-roh dwahzh ahplay poohr luh saiveess daytahzh)*

I'm leaving tomorrow
Je pars demain
(Zhuh pahr duhmung)

I need a wake-up call at 7 o'clock
Pouvez-vous me réveiller à 7 heures *(Poovay-voo muh rayvay-ay ah seterr)*

Do you arrange tours?
Est-ce que vous organisez des excursions? *(Esker voo zohrgahneezay day zexcewrsyong)*

Please prepare the bill
Pouvez-vous préparer ma note *(Poovay-voo praypahray mah not)*

There is a mistake in the bill
Il y a une erreur dans la note *(Illeeyah ewn airrerr dong lah not)*

What time must I vacate the room?
A quelle heure dois-je libérer la chambre?
(Ah kelerr dwazh leebayray lah shombr)

Can you call a taxi, please?
Pouvez-vous m'appeler un taxi, s'il vous plaît?
(Poovay-voo mahplay ung taxi, sillvooplay)

SELF-CATERING
APPARTEMENT-
HÔTEL

Have you any vacancies?
Avez-vous des unités libres? *(Avay-voo dayzewneetay leebr)*

How much is it per night/week?
Quel est le prix pour une nuit/à la semaine? *(Kel ay luh pree poohr ewn nwee/ah la suhmain)*

Do you allow children?
Vous acceptez les enfants? *(Voozakssayptay layzonfon)*

Please, show me how ... works
Pouvez-vous me montrer comment fonctionne ... *(Poovay voomuh montray commong fonksion ...)*

♦ **the water heater**
♦ le chauffe-eau *(luh showfoh)*

♦ **the dryer**
♦ le séchoir *(luh sayshwaar)*

♦ **the cooker/stove/ oven**
♦ la cuisinière/le four *(lah cwewzeenyair, luh foor)*

♦ **the washing machine**
♦ le lave-linge *(luh lahvlunzh)*

♦ **the heater**
♦ le chauffage *(luh showfazh)*

Where is/are ...?
Où est/sont ...? *(Oo ay/song ...)*

♦ **the switch**
♦ le bouton d'allumage *(luh bootong dallewmazh)*

♦ **the fuses**
♦ les fusibles *(lay fewzeebl)*

Is there ...?
Est-ce qu'il y a ...? *(Eskillya ...)*

♦ **a cot**
♦ un berceau *(ung bairsoh)*

♦ **a high chair**
♦ une chaise de bébé *(ewn shaiz duh baybay)*

♦ **a safe**
♦ un coffre-fort
   (ung coffruh fohr)

We need extra/ more ...
Il nous faudrait davantage de *(Eel noo fawdray davontazh duh)*

♦ **keys**
♦ clés *(clay)*

♦ **cutlery**
♦ couverts *(coovair)*

♦ **crockery**
♦ vaisselle *(vaissell)*

♦ **sheets**
♦ draps *(drah)*

♦ **blankets**
♦ couvertures
   (coovairtewr)

♦ **pillows**
♦ orelllers *(oraiyay)*

Is there ... in the vicinity?
Est-ce qu'il y a près d'ici? *(Eskillya praydeecee)*

♦ **a shop**
♦ un magasin
   (ung mahgahzung)

♦ **a restaurant**
♦ un restaurant
   (ung restaurong)

♦ **a bus/tram**
♦ un bus/un tramway
   (ung bews/tram)

I have locked myself out of my room
J'ai laissé la clé à l'intérieur de ma chambre
(Zhay layssay lah clay ah luntayryerr duh mah shombr)

The bathroom door is locked
La porte de la salle de bains est fermée à clé
(Lah port duh lah sal duh bung ay fairmmay ah clay)

The window won't open/close
La fenêtre ne s'ouvre pas/ne ferme pas *(Lah fuhnaytr nuh soovruh pah/nuh fairmuh pah)*

I enjoyed my stay, thank you
J'ai passé un séjour agréable, merci *(Zhai passay ung sayzhoor agrayahbl, mairsee)*

CAMPING
CAMPING

caravan
caravane *(caravan)*

Have you got a list of camp sites?
Avez-vous une liste des terrains de camping?
(Avay voo ewn leest day tayrung duh conpeen)

Are there any sites available?
Est-ce qu'il y a des places disponibles?
(Eskillya day plaas deesponeebl)

This site is muddy
Cet emplacement est boueux *(Setonplasmon ay boo-uh)*

Is there a sheltered site?
Est-ce qu'il y a un endroit abrité? *(Eskillya ung nondrwaa abreetay)*

Can we park the caravan here?
Est-ce qu'on peut parquer la caravane ici?
(Eskong puh parkay lah caravan eecee)

Can we camp here overnight?
Est-ce qu'on peut camper ici cette nuit?
(Eskong puh conpay eecee set nwee)

Is it safe for children?
Il n'y a pas de risques pour les enfants?
(Eelneeyah pah duh reesk poohr layzonfon)

Do you have electricity?
Est-ce qu'il y a l'électricité? *(Eskillya laylairktreeceeatay)*

Is there ... in the vicinity?
Est-ce qu'il ya près d'ici ...? *(Eskillya pray deecee)*

♦ a shop
♦ un magasin
(ung mahgahzung)

♦ a restaurant
♦ un restaurant
(ung restaurong)

♦ a picnic area
♦ une aire de pique-nique
(ewnair duh picnic)

46

We'd like to stay for ...
Nous désirons rester ...
(Noo dayseerong raystay)

◆ **three nights**
◆ trois nuits *(trwaa nwee)*

◆ **one week**
◆ une semaine
  (ewn suhmain)

Is there drinking water?
Est-ce qu'il y a de l'eau potable? *(Eskillya duh law pawtabl)*

Can I light a fire here?
Est-ce que je peux allumer un feu ici?
(Esker zhe puh allewmay ung fuh eecee)

I'd like to buy firewood
Je voudrais acheter du bois pour faire un feu
(Zhe voodray ashlay duh bwaa poohr fair dew fuh)

Is the wood dry?
Est-ce que le bois est sec?
(Esker luh bwaa ay sec)

Where is the nearest ...?
Où ...? *(Oo ...)*

◆ **toilet block**
◆ sont les toilettes
  (song lay twaalet)

◆ **shower**
◆ est la douche
  (ay lah douche)

◆ **sink (for washing dishes)**
◆ est l'évier *(ay layvyay)*

Do you have ... for rent?
Est-ce que vous pouvez me louer ...? *(Esker voo poovay muh lway ...)*

◆ **a tent**
◆ une tente *(ewn tont)*

◆ **a gas cylinder**
◆ une bouteille de gaz
  (ewn bootaiy duh gaaz)

◆ **a groundsheet**
◆ un tapis de sol
  (ung lahpee duh sol)

◆ **cooking utensils**
◆ des ustensils de cuisine
  (Dayzustonseel duh cweezeen)

◆ **saucepans**
◆ des casseroles
  (day cassroll)

CUTLERY
COUVERTS

knife
couteau *(cootow)*

fork
fourchette *(foorshet)*

spoon
cuillère *(cweeyair)*

crockery
vaisselle *(vaissail)*

plate
assiette *(assyait)*

cup and saucer
tasse et soucoupe
(tass ay soocoop)

mug
mug/gobelet *(mug/goblay)*

BREAKFAST
PETIT-DÉJEUNER

coffee ...
café ... *(cafay)*

- **with milk, cream**
- café au lait, café crème
  *(cafay oh lay,
  cafay craim)*

- **black**
- noir *(nwaar)*

- **without sugar**
- sans sucre
  (song sewcr)

tea ...
thé ... *(tay)*

- **with milk, lemon**
- au lait, au citron
  (oh lay, oh sitrong)

hot chocolate
chocolat chaud
(showcowlah show)

bread
pain *(pung)*

white bread
pain blanc *(pung blon)*

rye bread
pain de seigle
(pund duh saygl)

rolls
petits pains
(puhtee pung)

croissant
croissant *(crwasson)*

bun
brioche *(breeowsh)*

toast
toast *(toast)*

toasted bread
pain grillé *(pung greeyai)*

egg(s) ...
œuf(s) ... *(uhf)*

◆ **boiled – soft, hard**
◆ à la coque, dur(s)
(ah lah coc, dewr)

◆ **fried**
◆ au plat *(oh plah)*

◆ **scrambled**
◆ brouillé(s) *(brooyay)*

◆ **poached**
◆ poché(s) *(powshay)*

◆ **omelette**
◆ omelette *(omlet)*

bacon and eggs
œufs au bacon
(uhf oh baycon)

cereal
céréales *(sayray-al)*

hot milk, cold milk
lait chaud, lait froid
(lay show, frwaa)

fruit juice
jus de fruit
(zhew duh frwee)

fruit
fruit *(frwee)*

jam
confiture *(congfeetewr)*

marmalade
marmelade
(maarmuhlad)

butter
beurre *(berr)*

honey
miel *(myell)*

margarine
margarine *(margaareen)*

cold meats
charcuterie/viandes
froides *(sharcewtree,
vyond frwad)*

cheese
fromage *(frowmazh)*

pepper
poivre *(pwavr)*

salt
sel *(sell)*

sugar
sucre *(sewcr)*

oil and vinegar
huile et vinaigre
(weel ay veenaygr)

LUNCH/DINNER
DÉJEUNER/DÎNER

Could we have a table ...?
Peut-on avoir une table ...? *(Puhtong aavwaar ewn tabl ...)*

◆ **by the window**
◆ près de la fenêtre *(pray duh lah fuhnaytr)*

◆ **outside**
◆ dehors *(duh-orr)*

◆ **inside**
◆ à l'intérieur *(ah luntayryerr)*

◆ **for four people**
◆ pour quatre *(poohr catr)*

May I have ... please?
S'il vous plaît ...? *(Sillvooplay)*

◆ **the menu**
◆ le menu *(luh muhnew)*

◆ **the wine list**
◆ la carte des vins *(lah cart day vung)*

◆ **starters**
◆ hors-d'œuvre *(orrduhvr)*

◆ **main course**
◆ plat principal *(plah prungseepahl)*

◆ **dessert**
◆ dessert *(daysser)*

What is the dish of the day?
Quel est le plat du jour? *(Kel ay luh plah dew zhoor)*

I'll take the set menu
Je vais prendre le menu fixe *(Zhe vay prondr luh muhnew feex)*

What is this?
Ça, qu'est-ce que c'est? *(Sa, kesker say)*

That is not what I ordered
Je n'ai pas commandé ça *(Zhe nay pah comonday sa)*

It is tough, cold
C'est dur, froid *(Say dewr, frwaa)*

What do you recommend?
Qu'est-ce que vous conseillez? *(Kesker voo consaiyay)*

Can I have the bill, please?
L'addition, s'il vous plaît
(*Lahdeesiong, sillvooplay*)

Could we have some water?
Est-ce que nous pourrions avoir de l'eau?
(*Esker noo poohryong aavwar duh low*)

We'd like to pay separately
Des additions séparées, s'il vous plaît
(*Dayzadeesiong saypahray, sill voo play*)

How much is it?
Ça fait combien?
(*Sa fay combyah*)

Is service included?
Le service est compris?
(*Luh sairveess ay conpree*)

There is a mistake
Il y a une erreur
(*Eelyah ewn erruhr*)

Thanks, that's for you
Merci, voilà pour vous
(*Mairsee, vwalah poohr voo*)

Keep the change
Gardez la monnaie
(*gaarday lah monnay*)

FAST FOOD/ TAKEAWAYS
FAST FOOD/PLATS À EMPORTER

pizza
pizza (*pizza*)

ham sandwich
sandwich au jambon
(*sondweesh oh zhonbong*)

toasted ham and cheese
croque-monsieur
(*croc-muhsyew*)

hot dog
hot dog (*ot dog*)

DRINKS
POUR BOIRE

a beer/lager (large)
une bière brune/blonde, un demi (*Ewn byair brewn/ blond, ung duhmee*)

draught beer
bière à la pression
(*byair ah lah pressiong*)

a glass, a bottle
un verre, une bouteille
(*ung vair, ewn bootaiy*)

dry white wine
un vin blanc sec
(*ung vung blon sec*)

sweet white wine
un vin blanc doux
(*ung vung blong doo*)

red wine
vin rouge (*vung roozh*)

new wine
vin nouveau
(*vung noovoh*)

house wine
vin de pays
(*vung duh payee*)

a brandy
un brandy/Cognac
(*ung brondee/Coñac*)

a whisky with/without ice
un whisky avec/sans
glaçons (*ung weeskee
aavayk/song glaasong*)

a mineral water – still, sparkling
une eau minérale – plate,
gazeuse (*ewnoh mee-
nayral – plaat, gaazuhz*)

tap water
eau du robinet
(*oh dew rohbeenay*)

tomato juice
jus de tomate
(*zhuh duh tohmat*)

a glass of Champagne
une coupe de
Champagne (*ewn
coop duh shonpañ*)

a glass of cider
un verre de cidre
(*ung vair duh sidr*)

ice tea
thé glacé (*tay glaassay*)

shandy
panaché (*panaashay*)

clear spirit
alcool (*alcol*)

liqueur
liqueur (*likerr*)

punch
punch (*ponsh*)

another, please
un autre, s'il vous plaît
(*unowtr, sillvooplay*)

too cold
trop froid (*troh frwaa*)

not cold enough
pas assez froid
(*pah assay frwaa*)

FOOD
POUR MANGER

SOUP, CREAM SOUP
SOUPE, VELOUTÉ
(soop, vuhlootay)

mushroom soup, tomato soup
velouté de champignons, tomate *(vuhlootay de shonpeeñong, tohmat)*

vegetable soup
potage *(pohtazh)*

consommé
consommé *(consomay)*

beef broth, chicken broth
bouillon de bœuf, de poulet *(Booyong duh buhf, duh poolay)*

FISH
POISSON *(pwassong)*

sole
sole *(sol)*

cod
cabillaud *(cabeeyoh)*

salmon
saumon *(sohmong)*

herring
hareng *(aarong)*

trout
truite *(trweet)*

tuna
thon *(tong)*

fried, grilled, poached
frit, grillé, poché *(free, greeyay, poshay)*

oysters
huîtres *(weetr)*

POULTRY
VOLAILLE *(vohlaiy)*

chicken
poulet *(poolay)*

duck
canard *(cahnaar)*

goose
oie *(waa)*

roasted
rôti *(rohtee)*

MEAT
VIANDE *(vyond)*

veal
veau *(vow)*

mutton, lamb
mouton, agneau
(mootong, aañow)

beef
bœuf *(buhf)*

pork
porc *(pohr)*

sausage
saucisse *(sawsseess)*

vienna, frankfurter
saucisse de Vienne, de
Francfort *(sawsseess
duh Vyain, duh Froncfor)*

venison
venaison *(vuhnaysong)*

steak
bifteck *(beeftayk)*

**well-done, medium,
rare**
bien cuit, à point, saignant
*(byah cwee, ah pwung,
sayñon)*

platter of cold meats
assiette de charcuterie/
viandes froides *(ahssyet
duh sharcewtree/vyond
frwad)*

blood sausage
boudin *(boodung)*

pasta
pâtes *(paat)*

rice
riz *(ree)*

VEGETABLES
LÉGUMES *(laygewm)*

cauliflower
chou-fleur *(shoo-fluhr)*

carrots
carottes *(caroht)*

leek
poireau *(pwahrow)*

asparagus
asperges *(asperzh)*

peppers
poivrons *(pwavrong)*

green beans
haricots verts
(aareecoh vair)

potatoes
pommes de terre
(pom duh tair)

boiled, fried, mashed
en robe des champs,
frites, purée
*(ong rohb day shon,
freet, pewray)*

SALAD
SALADE *(salad)*

lettuce
laitue *(laytew)*

beetroot
betterave *(bettrav)*

cucumber
concombre *(congcongbr)*

tomato
tomate *(tohmat)*

root celery
céleri rémoulade
(saylree raymoolad)

FRUIT
FRUITS *(frwee)*

fruit salad
salade de fruits
(salad duh frwee)

apple
pomme *(pom)*

pear
poire *(pwaar)*

banana
banane *(bahnahn)*

redcurrant
groseille rouge
(growsaiy roozh)

blackcurrant
cassis *(casseess)*

pineapple
ananas *(ahnahnass)*

**passion fruit/
grenadilla**
fruit de la passion/
grenadine *(frwee duh lah
passiong/gruhnahdeen)*

apricot
abricot *(ahbreecoh)*

peach
pêche *(paysh)*

strawberry
fraise *(frayz)*

raspberry
framboise *(fronbwaz)*

blackberry
mûre *(mewr)*

blueberry
myrtille *(meerteey)*

prune
pruneau *(pruhnoh)*

plum
prune *(prewn)*

dried fruits
fruits secs *(frwee sec)*

DESSERT/CAKES
DESSERT/PÂTISSERIE

chocolate mousse
mousse au chocolat
(mooss oh showcowlah)

apple/fruit tart
tarte aux pommes/fruits
(tart oh pom/frwee)

caramel cream
crème caramel
(craim caramol)

crème brûlée
crème brûlée
(craim brewlay)

custard
crème anglaise
(craim onglayz)

apple upside down tart
tarte Tatin *(tart Tahtung)*

profiteroles
profiteroles *(prowfeetrole)*

meringues
meringues *(muhrung)*

coffee ice cream with whipped cream
café liégeois
(cafay leeayzhwah)

coffee ice cream
glace au café
(glaass oh cafay)

water ice
sorbet *(sorbay)*

lemon/fruit sorbet
sorbet au citron/aux fruits
*(sorbay oh sitrong/
oh frwee)*

cheese
fromage *(frowmazh)*

coffee
café *(cafay)*

black coffee
café noir *(cafay nwaar)*

white coffee
café crème *(cafay craim)*

filter coffee
café filtre *(cafay feeltr)*

espresso
express *(express)*

decaffeinated coffee
café décaféiné
(cafay daycafay-eenay)

cappuccino
cappuccino
(capoochinnoh)

MONEY MATTERS
FINANCES

Where can I change money?
Où est-ce que je peux changer de l'argent?
(Oo esker zhuh puh shonzhay duh larzhong)

Where is ...?
Où est-ce qu'il y a ...?
(Oo eskillya ...)

◆ **an ATM/cash machine**
◆ une billetterie *(ewn beeyaytree)*

◆ **a bank**
◆ une banque *(ewn bonk)*

◆ **a bureau de change**
◆ un bureau de change *(ung burow duh shonzh)*

When does the bank open/close?
A quelle heure ouvre/ferme la banque? *(Ah kelerr oovruh/fairmuh lah bonk)*

What's the rate for ...?
Quel est le taux de change ...? *(Kelay luh tow duh shonzh ...)*

◆ **dollars, pounds, euros**
◆ du dollar, de la livre-sterling, de l'euro *(dew dowlaar, duh lah leevruh stairleeñ, duh luhrow)*

How much commission do you charge?
A combien s'élève votre commission? *(Ah combyah saylayv votruh comeesiong)*

I want to ...
Je voudrais ...
(zhuh voodray ...)

◆ **cash a traveller's cheque**
◆ encaisser un traveller's chèque *(oncayssay ung trahvuhlerr shek)*

◆ **change £50**
◆ changer 50 livres *(shonzhay suncont leevr)*

◆ **make a transfer/ a remittance**
◆ effectuer un transfert/ un paiement *(ayfayctway ung tronsfair/ung paymon)*

POST OFFICE
BUREAU DE POSTE

How much is ...?
Quel est le prix pour envoyer ...? *(Kelay luh pree poohr onvwayay)*

◆ **a letter to ...**
◆ une lettre en ... *(ewn lettr on ...)*

◆ **a postcard to ...**
◆ une carte postale en ... *(ewn cart postaal on ...)*

◆ **a small parcel to ...**
◆ un petit colis en ... *(ung puhtee cowlee on ...)*

airmail
par avion *(paaraavyong)*

Where can I buy stamps?
Où est-ce que je peux acheter des timbres? *(Oo esker zhuh puh ashtay day tungbr)*

SHOPPING
LES ACHATS

Where do I pay?
Je paie où? *(zhu pay oo)*

cash desk
caisse *(kess)*

What does it cost?
Ça coûte combien? *(Sa coot combya)*

I need a receipt
J'ai besoin d'un reçu *(Zhay buhzwung dung ruhssew)*

Do you accept credit cards?
Vous acceptez les cartes de crédit? *(Voozaksayptay lay cart duh craydee)*

Does it include VAT?
La TVA est incluse? *(Lah tayvay-ah aytunclew)*

Do you need a deposit?
Vous voulez un acompte/ des arrhes? *(Voo voolay unahcont/dayzahr)*

This is not what I want
Ce n'est pas ce que je veux *(suh nay pah suh kuh zuh vuh)*

I want my money back
Je veux être remboursé(e) *(Zhu vuh airtruh ronboorsay)*

I want to complain
Je veux me plaindre à la direction *(Zhu vuh muh plundr ah lah deereksiong)*

Can you wrap it up?
Pouvez-vous me l'envelopper? *(Poovay voo muh lonvlohpay)*

It is ...
C'est ... *(Say)*

♦ **damaged**
♦ abîmé *(ahbeemay)*

♦ **old/stale**
♦ vieux/rassis *(vyuh/ rahsee)*

Can you repair it?
C'est réparable/vous pouvez le réparer? *(Say raypahrabl/poovay voo luh raypahray)*

GROCERY SHOPPING
ACHATS D'EPICERIE

Where can I buy ...?
Où peut-on acheter ...? *(Oo puhtong ashtay ...)*

♦ **bread**
♦ du pain *(du pung)*

♦ **cakes**
♦ des gâteaux *(day gahtoh)*

♦ **cheese**
♦ du fromage *(dew frohmazh)*

♦ **butter**
♦ du beurre *(dew buhrr)*

♦ **milk**
♦ du lait *(dew lay)*

♦ **mineral water**
♦ de l'eau minérale *(duh loh meenayrahl)*

♦ **wine**
♦ du vin *(dew vung)*

♦ **beer**
♦ de la bière *(duh lah byair)*

♦ **fruit juice**
♦ du jus de fruit *(dew zhewd frwee)*

♦ **meat**
♦ de la viande *(duh lah vyond)*

♦ **cold meats**
♦ de la charcuterie *(duh lah sharcewtree)*

♦ **eggs**
♦ des œufs *(daysuh)*

- **fruit, vegetables**
- des fruits, des légumes
  (day frwee, day laygewm)

I'd like ...
Je voudrais ...
  (Zhu voodray ...)

- **three slices**
- trois tranches
  (trwah tronsh)

- **a portion of ...**
- un morceau/une portion de ...
  (Ung mohrsoh/ ewn porsyong duh ...)

- **a packet of ...**
- un paquet de ...
  (ung pahkay duh ...)

- **a can/tin of ...**
- une boîte de ...
  (ewn bwaht duh ...)

- **a bottle of ...**
- une bouteille de ...
  (ewn bootaiy duh ...)

- **a dozen ...**
- une douzaine de ...
  (ewn doozain duh ...)

- **a jar of ...**
- un bocal de ...
  (ung bohcahl duh ...)

BUYING CLOTHES
ACHATS DE VÊTEMENTS

Can I try this on?
Je peux essayer ça?
  (zuh puh ayssay-yai sah)

It is ...
C'est ... *(Say)*

- **too big**
- trop grand *(troh grong)*

- **too small**
- trop petit *(troh puhtee)*

- **too tight**
- trop serré *(troh sairray)*

- **too wide**
- trop large *(troh larzh)*

- **too expensive**
- trop cher *(troh shair)*

I'll take ...
Je prends ...
  (zhu prong ...)

- **this one**
- celui-là/celle-là
  (suhlwee-lah/sell-lah)

- **size 42**
- le 42 *(luh caront-duh)*

CLOTHING SIZES – TAILLES DES VÊTEMENTS

Women's Wear

UK	Cont. Europe	USA
10	36	8
12	38	10
14	40	12
16	42	14
18	44	16

Menswear

UK	Cont. Europe	USA
36	46	36
38	48	38
40	50	40
42	52	42
44	54	44
46	56	46

Men's Shirts

UK	Cont. Europe	USA
14	36	14
14.5	37	14.5
15	38	15
15.5	39	15.5
16	40	16
17	42	17

Shoes

UK	Cont. Europe	USA
5	38	6
6	39	7
7	40	8
8	42	9
9	43	10
10	44	11
11	45	12

SIGHTSEEING
TOURISME

tourist office
office du tourisme/syndicat d'initiative *(ohfeess duh tooreesm/sundeecah deeneesiahteev)*

Do you have brochures/leaflets?
Vous avez des brochures? *(Voozavay day brohshewr)*

I/We want to visit ...
Je veux/nous voulons visiter ... *(Zhuh vuh/noo voolong veeseetay ...)*

When is it open/closed?
Quelles sont les heures d'ouverture/de fermeture? *(Kel song layzerr doovair-tewr/de fairmuhtewr)*

What does it cost?
Ça coûte combien? *(Sah coot combyah)*

Are there any reductions for ...?
Est-ce qu'il y a des prix spéciaux pour ...? *(Eskillya day pree spaysyoh poohr ...)*

◆ children
◆ les enfants *(layzonfon)*

◆ students
◆ les étudiants *(lay zaytewdyong)*

◆ senior citizens
◆ les retraités *(lay ruhtraytay)*

Are there any sightseeing tours?
Est-ce qu'il y a des excursions organisées? *(Eskillya day zayscewrsyong ohrgahneezay)*

When does the coach depart/return?
A quelle heure part/revient le car? *(Ah kelerr pahr/ruhvyah luh cahr)*

Are meals, entrance fees included?
Est-ce que repas et prix d'entrée sont compris? *(Esker ruhpah ay pree dontray song conpree)*

Where is the museum?
Où est le musée? *(Oo ay luh mewzay)*

ENTERTAINMENT
DISTRACTIONS

Is there a list of cultural events?
Avez-vous une liste des activités culturelles?
(Avay-voo ewn leest day zacteeveetay cewltewrel)

Are there festivals?
Est-ce qu'il y a des festivals? *(Eskillya day festeevahl)*

I'd like to go to ...
Je voudrais aller ...
(Zuh voodray allay ...)

◆ **the theatre**
◆ au théâtre *(oh tayahtr)*

◆ **the opera**
◆ à l'opéra *(ah lohpayrah)*

◆ **the cinema/movies**
◆ au cinéma
(oh cinaymah)

◆ **a concert**
◆ au concert
(oh conssair)

What is on/showing?
Qu'est-ce qu'on joue?
(Kesskong zhooh)

Do I have to book?
Est-ce qu'il faut réserver?
(Eskillfoh raysaivay)

Two tickets for ...
Deux billets pour ...
(Duh beeyay poohr ...)

◆ **tonight**
◆ ce soir *(suh swahr)*

◆ **the early show**
◆ la première séance
(lah pruhmyair sayahns)

◆ **the late show**
◆ la dernière séance
(la dairnyair sayahns)

When does the performance start/end?
A quelle heure commence/finit la séance?
(Ah keluhr cohmons/feenee la sayahns)

Where is ...?
Où est-ce qu'il y a ...?
(Oo eskillya ...)

◆ **a good bar**
◆ un bon bar
(ung bong bar)

◆ **a good disco**
◆ une bonne discothèque *(ewn bonn deescohteck)*

- **a good band**
- un bon orchestre
  (ung bonn orkairstre)

- **a soccer match**
- un match de football
  (ung mahtch duh footbohl)

Is it ...?
Est-ce que c'est ...?
(Eskersay)

- **expensive**
- cher *(shair)*

- **crowded**
- plein de monde
  (plung duh mond)

How do I get there?
Comment est-ce que je peux y aller? *(Commong esker zhuh puh ee ahlay)*

SPORT
SPORT

Where can we ...?
Où est-ce que nous pouvons ...? *(Oo esker noo poovong ...)*

- **play tennis**
- jouer au tennis
  (zhooay oh tayneess)

- **play golf**
- jouer au golf
  (zhoouay oh golf)

- **go skiing**
- faire du ski
  (fairr dew skee)

- **go swimming**
- nager *(nahzhay)*

- **go fishing**
- aller à la pêche
  (allay ah lah pairsh)

- **go riding**
- faire du cheval
  (fairr dew shuhvahl)

- **go cycling**
- faire du vélo
  (fairr dew vayloh)

- **hire bicycles**
- louer des vélos
  (lway day vayloh)

- **hire golf clubs**
- louer des clubs de golf
  (lway day club duh golf)

- **hire skis**
- louer des skis
  (lway day skee)

- **hire a boat**
- louer un bateau
  (lway ung bahtoh)

How much is it ...?
Quel est le prix calculé ...?
(Kelay luh pree calcewlay)

- ◆ **per hour/day**
- ◆ à l'heure/à la journée
  (ah lerr/ah lah zhoornay)

- ◆ **per session/game**
- ◆ par séance/jeu
  (pahr saiyonss/zuh)

Is it ...?
Est-ce que c'est ...?
(Esker say ...)

- ◆ **safe**
- ◆ sans danger
  (song dongzhay)

- ◆ **deep**
- ◆ profond *(prohfong)*

How do we get there?
Comment est-ce que
nous pouvons y aller?
*(Commong esker noo
poovong eeyallay)*

no swimming
défense de nager
(dayfons duh nahzhay)

no diving
défense de plonger
(dayfons duh plongzhay)

danger
danger *(donzhay)*

Are there currents?
Est-ce qu'il y a des
courants?
(Eskillya day coorong)

Do I need a fishing permit?
Est-ce que j'ai besoin
d'un permis de pêche?
*(Esker zhay buhzwa
dung pairmee duh pairsh)*

Where can I get one?
Où est-ce que je peux en
obtenir un? *(Oo esker zhuh
puh onobtuhneer ung)*

Is there a guide for walks?
Est-ce qu'il y a un guide
pour les randonnées?
*(Eskillya ung geed poohr
lay rondonay)*

Where is the nearest sport shop?
Où est la boutique de
sport la plus proche?
*(Oo ay lah booteek duh
spohr lah plew prosh)*

I am a beginner
Je suis débutant(e)
*(Zhuh swee daybewtong/
daybewtont)*

How much is a ski pass?
Combien coûte un laisser-passer pour le ski? *(Combyah coot ung layssay-passay poohr luh skee)*

Is there a map of the ski runs?
Est-ce qu'il y a une carte des pistes de ski? *(Eskillya ewn cart day peestuh duh skee)*

Is it safe to ski today?
On peut skier sans danger aujourd'hui? *(Ong puh skyay song donzhay ohzhoordwee)*

Which is an easy run?
Où est-ce qu'il y a une piste facile? *(Oo eskillya ewn peest fahseel)*

Where can we go cross-country skiing?
Où est-ce qu'on peut faire du ski de fond? *(Oo eskong puh fair dew skee duh fong)*

My skis are too long/too short
Mes skis sont trop longs/trop courts *(May skee song troh long/troh coor)*

Is there a ski lift?
Est-ce qu'il y a un télésiège? *(Eskillya ung taylaysyaizh)*

run closed
piste fermée *(peestuh fairmay)*

avalanches
avalanches *(ahvahlonsh)*

We want to go ...
Nous voulons faire ... *(Noo voolong fair ...)*

- **hiking**
- une randonnée *(ewn rondonay)*

- **canoeing**
- du canoë *(dew cahnohay)*

- **mountaineering**
- de l'alpinisme *(dul lahlpeeneesm)*

- **sailing**
- de la voile *(duh lah vwahl)*

- **water-skiing**
- du ski nautique *(dew skee nohteek)*

- **ice-skating**
- du patin à glace *(dew pahtung ah glass)*

PHARMACY/ CHEMIST
PHARMACIE (green cross on white sign)

Have you got something for ...?
Avez-vous quelque chose pour ...? *(Avay voo kelkuh shohz poohr ...)*

- **diarrhoea**
- la diarrhée *(lah dyahray)*

- **headache**
- les maux de tête *(lay moh duh tait)*

- **nausea**
- la nausée *(lah nohsay)*

- **a sore throat**
- le mal de gorge *(luh mahl duh gorzh)*

- **a cold or flu**
- le rhume ou la grippe *(luh rewm oo lah greep)*

- **hay fever**
- le rhume des foins *(luh rewm day fwung)*

I need ...
Je voudrais ... *(Zhuh voodray ...)*

- **indigestion tablets**
- quelque chose pour l'indigestion *(kelkuh shohz poohr lundeezhestyong)*

- **a laxative**
- un laxatif *(ung lahksahteef)*

- **sleeping tablets**
- un somnifère *(ung sohmneefair)*

Is it safe for children?
Ça convient pour un enfant? *(Sa convya poohr unonfon)*

I'm on this medication
Je prends ce médicament *(Zhuh prong se maydeecahmong)*

I am a diabetic
Je suis diabétique *(Zhuh swee deeahbayteek)*

I am pregnant
Je suis enceinte *(Zhe swee onsent)*

I'm on the pill
Je prends un contraceptif/ la pilule *(Zhuh prong ung contrahsepteef/ lah peelewl)*

I'm allergic to ...
Je suis allergique à ... *(Zhuh swee ahlairzheek ah ...)*

I have high blood pressure
J'ai de l'hypertension *(Zhay duh leepairtonsyong)*

DOCTOR
CHEZ LE MÉDECIN

I am ill
Je suis malade
(Zhuh swee mahlahd)

I need a doctor
Je veux voir un médecin
(Zhuh vuh vwahr ung maydsung)

He/she has a high temperature
Il/elle a beaucoup de température *(eel/ell ah bohcoo duh tahmpayrahtewr)*

It hurts
Ça fait mal/c'est douloureux *(Sah fay mahl/say doolooruh)*

I've been vomiting
J'ai vomi *(Zhay vohmee)*

I have toothache
J'ai mal aux dents
(Zhay mahl oh dong)

Dentist
Dentiste *(Donteest)*

Ophthalmologist
Ophtalmologiste
(Ophtahlmohlogeest)

HOSPITAL
HÔPITAL

Will I have to go to hospital?
Je dois être hospitalisé(e)? *(Zhuh dwah aytrohspeetahleesay)*

Where's the hospital?
Où est l'hôpital?
(Oo ay lohpeetahl)

Which ward?
Quelle salle? *(Kel sahl)*

When are visiting hours?
Quelles sont les heures de visite? *(Kel song lay zerr duh veeseet)*

Where is casualty?
Où est le service des urgences? *(Oo ay luh sairvees day zewrzhons)*

How much will it cost?
Combien est-ce que ça va coûter? *(Conbyah esker sah vah cootay)*

POLICE
POLICE

Call the police
Appelez la police *(Ahplay lah pohlees)*

I have been robbed
J'ai été victime d'un vol *(Zhai aytay veecteem dung vohl)*

My car has been stolen
Ma voiture a été volée *(Mah vwahtewr ah aytay vohlay)*

My car has been broken into
Ma voiture a été cambriolée *(Mah vwahtewr ah aytay conbreeohlay)*

I want to report a theft
Je voudrais déclarer un vol *(Zhuh voodray dayclahray ung vohl)*

I have been raped
J'ai été violée *(Zhay aytay veeohlay)*

Where is the police station?
Où est le commissariat de police/la gendarmerie? *(Oo ay luh commeessahryah duh pohlees/lah zhondarmuhree)*

EMERGENCIES
URGENCES

Call an ambulance
Appelez une ambulance *(Ahplay ewn onbewlons)*

There has been an accident
Il y a eu un accident *(Eel-yah ew ung nakseedon)*

Someone is injured
Quelqu'un est blessé *(Kelkung ay blayssay)*

Help!
Au secours! *(Ohscoor!)*

My son/daughter is missing
Mon fils/ma fille a disparu *(Mong fees/mah feey ah dispahrew)*

Hurry up!
Vite! Dépêchez-vous!
(Veet! Daypayshay-voo!)

This is an emergency!
C'est une urgence!
(Say tewn ewrzhons)

Can I have a receipt for my insurance?
Puis-je avoir un reçu pour mon assurance? *(Pweezh ahvvahr ung ruhssew poohr monassewrons)*

These are my insurance details
Vioci les coordonnées de mon assurance *(Vwahsee lay co-hordohnay duh monassewrons)*

I have to use the telephone
Il faut que je téléphone *(Eel foh kuh zhuh taylayphon)*

Can anyone here speak English?
Est-ce qu'il y a quelqu'un ici qui parle anglais? *(Eskillyah kelkung eesee kee parlonglay)*

I am lost
Je suis perdu(e) *(Zhuh swee pairdew)*

FIRE DEPARTMENT
POMPIERS

Fire!
Au feu! *(Ohfuh!)*

Look out!
Attention! *(Ahtonsyon!)*

Call the fire department
Appelez les pompiers
(Ahplay lay pongpyay)

The fire is on the third floor of the hotel
L'incendie est au troisième étage de l'hôtel *(Lunsondee aytoh trwahzyem aytazh duh lohtel)*

The address is ...
L'adresse est ...
(Lahdress ay ...)

I need ...
J'ai besoin ...
(Zhay buhzwung ...)

♦ **a fire extinguisher**
♦ d'un extincteur
  (dung extunktuhr)

♦ **medical assistance**
♦ d'assistance médicale
  (dassistons maydeecahl)

THE HUMAN BODY
LE CORPS HUMAIN

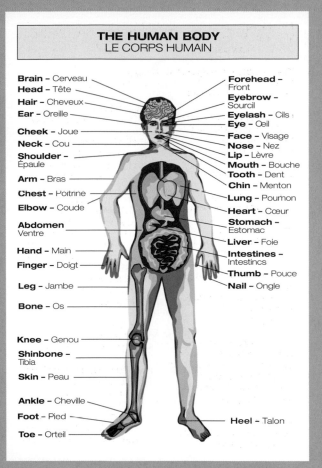

Brain – Cerveau
Head – Tête
Hair – Cheveux
Ear – Oreille
Cheek – Joue
Neck – Cou
Shoulder – Épaule
Arm – Bras
Chest – Poitrine
Elbow – Coude
Abdomen – Ventre
Hand – Main
Finger – Doigt
Leg – Jambe
Bone – Os
Knee – Genou
Shinbone – Tibia
Skin – Peau
Ankle – Cheville
Foot – Pied
Toe – Orteil

Forehead – Front
Eyebrow – Sourcil
Eyelash – Cils
Eye – Œil
Face – Visage
Nose – Nez
Lip – Lèvre
Mouth – Bouche
Tooth – Dent
Chin – Menton
Lung – Poumon
Heart – Cœur
Stomach – Estomac
Liver – Foie
Intestines – Intestincs
Thumb – Pouce
Nail – Ongle

Heel – Talon

75

FORMS OF ADDRESS
TITRES ET FORMES

There is a marked difference in approach to 'etiquette' (the way to behave in polite society) between the older and the younger generation of French people. Whereas the former would adhere strictly to the polite form of address – *vous* – until such time as it is mutually agreed to progress to the familiar *tu*, the younger generation tends to adopt the more familiar *tu* form far more readily. One should tread warily here – the fact that you may be invited to call someone by his/her first name does not automatically imply the use of the familiar *tu*. Young people are far more casual about this among themselves (especially in an informal context), but will generally adhere to the polite form when addressing older people, or when they meet in a business environment, or speak to shop assistants, etc.

The correct form of address – *Monsieur* and *Madame* (*Mademoiselle* is rarely used these days) – implies that the person to whom you are speaking is an adult, either male or female, and that you are on polite terms. *Docteur* is exclusively an academic title and used only for a doctor in medicine. An advocate will be addressed as *Maître*, a cabinet minister as *Monsieur le Ministre* or *Madame la Ministre*, and a university professor as *Professeur*.

GREETINGS
SALUTATIONS

Like forms of address, forms of greeting also tend to vary among the older and younger generations. Whereas it is correct to say *Bonjour* and *Bonsoir*, young people will often greet each other simply by saying *Salut!* for 'hello' and *Ciao!* for 'goodbye', and a handshake will very often be replaced by up to three kisses on the cheeks, alternating between left and right.

When you are introduced to somebody in a formal context, such as a business meeting, the correct greeting would be *Enchanté(e)* ('Pleased to meet you'), but a simple *Bonjour* ('Good day') will generally suffice in a more informal situation.

THANK YOU
REMERCIEMENTS

When you are invited to a meal in a private home it is appropriate for you to bring flowers for the hostess, but make sure you don't bring chrysanthemums, as these are the flowers traditionally used to decorate tombs on All Saints' Day. (If you are on more intimate terms with your hostess, chocolates or wine can be substituted for the flowers). The *Merci beaucoup* ('Thank you very much') extended by you on leaving should be followed up with a phone call the next day.

When somebody thanks you, you should answer: *Je vous en prie* ('It's a pleasure'). An alternative to this is: *de rien* ('Don't mention it') which is quite frequently used although not particularly elegant.

MANNERS
BONNES MANIÈRES

Punctuality is absolutely expected but with a reasonable margin to cater for possible traffic problems in congested cities. So if you're going to meet someone, it would be worth your while to leave a little earlier than you think is necessary, especially if you're not sure of the route.

There are some things you should not do when dining in a French restaurant. The atmosphere is usually rather elegant, so raucous behaviour and loud talking don't go down very well. Don't ask for a doggy bag in France, as this is not the custom here. Try to order your meal in French – this will be appreciated by your waiter. And finally, despite what you've seen in the movies, it is not the done thing to refer to your waiter as *garçon*, which means 'boy' and is considered to be derogatory.

The expression *Bon appétit* (which could be translated as 'Enjoy your meal') should be used sparingly and is best reserved for meals with family and friends.

The same reservation applies for the expression that is frequently used in English when someone sneezes – 'Bless you!'. The polite response to a sneeze is simply to ignore it. The person who has sneezed will quietly say *Pardon!*

DRIVING
AU VOLANT

Remember that in France, like in the rest of continental Europe, you drive on the right-hand side of the road. Although there is a universal kind of 'etiquette' which encompasses respect for the driving code and being courteous to the other road users, it might be useful to note a difference in the interpretation of the flashing of headlights – in France this is a warning of danger or a way to show your disapproval, and NOT an invitation to have priority of passage.

Speeding fines can be rather substantial, so it would be a good idea to stick to the speed limits. Depending on whether you are in France, Switzerland, Belgium or Canada, and also depending on weather conditions, the speed limit on toll roads and motorways is between 100 and 130 kilometres per hour, on other roads outside built-up areas it is between 80 and 100 kilometres per hour, and in cities and towns it varies from 50 to 60 kilometres per hour. If in doubt, it is better to slow down.

OFFICIAL HOLIDAYS
JOURS FÉRIÉS

New Year's Eve and New Year's Day
Saint-Sylvestre (31 December), *Jour de l'An* (1 January)
Exuberant parties and dances are held on 31 December – *Saint-Sylvestre* – so most people spend New Year's Day recovering quietly. In Switzerland, 2 January (Epiphany or Second New Year's Day) is also a holiday.

Easter *Pâques* (Easter Sunday and Easter Monday)
Special church services are held. Of course there are also Easter Eggs for the children, including hand-painted hard-boiled eggs.

Ascension Day
Ascension (May)
This religious holiday is celebrated in France, Belgium and Switzerland.

Pentecost
Pentecôte (May/June, Sunday and Monday)
A religious holiday in France, Switzerland and Belgium.

Christmas Day, St Stephen's Day
Noël (25 December), *Saint-Etienne* (26 December)
Christmas Day is celebrated with church

services and giving of gifts. In Switzerland St Stephen's Day (26 December) is also a public holiday.

REGIONAL HOLIDAYS
FÊTES RÉGIONALES

Labour Day
Fête du Travail (1 May)
Celebrated in France, especially for workers. There are parades and festivities.

Victory Day
Fête de la Libération (8 May)
This holiday celebrates the liberation of France in 1945 at the end of World War II. Various ceremonies are held around France to mark this day.

Assumption Day
Assomption (15 August)
Special church services are held in France and Belgium on Assumption Day.

All Saints' Day
Toussaint (1 November)
A religious holiday in France and Belgium.

Armistice Day
Armistice (11 November)
Ceremonies are held in France and Belgium on this holiday.

Festival of Lights
(8 December)
Held in Lyon (near the French Alps), this religious festival celebrates the Virgin Mary with candle-lit windows.

NATIONAL DAYS
FÊTES NATIONALES

Bastille Day
(14 July) The National Day of France, Bastille Day (Independence Day) is celebrated with parades and fireworks.

Fête Nationale
(21 July) Independence Day, the National Day of Belgium, also features parades and fireworks.

Fête Nationale
(1 August) The National Day of Switzerland.

Fête Nationale
(June) Although Canada Day (1 July) is Canada's official National Day, the province of Quebec has its own 'national' holiday. This is called the *Fête Nationale*, and is celebrated on the Monday falling the closest to 24 June. This is the feast of St John the Baptist, and the day was formerly referred to as St Jean-Baptiste.

SPECIAL FESTIVALS
FÊTES SPECIALES

Carnival
(February/March) This special festival takes place in Nice on the French Riviera, and consists of Mardi Gras, parades, flower processions and fireworks.

Lemon Festival
(February/March)

Running at the same time as the Carnival in Nice, and also located on the French Riviera, the Lemon Festival at Menton has various parades, music, fireworks and an art exhibition.

Sechseläuten
(April)

This spring festival, held in Zürich in Switzerland, has colourful parades and the burning of a 'winter' effigy to welcome the approach of spring.

Cannes Film Festival
(May)

This world-famous film festival, brimming with movie stars, takes place every year at Cannes on the French Riviera.

Fête de la Musique
(21 June)

Anybody who can play a musical instrument is encouraged to play in the street late into the night.

Military Parades
(14 July)

All over France, people dance in the streets the whole night long.

Summer Festival
(June/July)

Various concerts and other events take place in Brussels in Belgium.

Ommegang
(July)
This medieval pageant takes place in Brussels, Belgium.

Music Festivals
(June–August)
A variety of summer music festivals are held throughout France during the summer each year.

Flower Festival
(August)
This festival is held in Brussels every other year in the even-numbered years. During the festival, Grand Place square is carpeted with hundreds of thousands of flowers, making a spectacular display.

Festivals of Flanders
(September/October)
Various international concerts are presented in the medieval atmosphere of several abbeys, the cathedral and the town hall of Ghent in Belgium.

Festival of Colours
(October)
You can celebrate the magnificent colours of the fall (autumn) foliage at Rigaud, near Montreal in Quebec, Canada.

Onion Market Fair
(November)
A traditional farmer's market held in Bern in Switzerland, with jesters and confetti 'battles'.

ENGLISH → FRENCH

A

abbey abbaye f

abortion avortement m

about (approximately) plus ou moins, approximativement

above au dessus

abroad à l'étranger

abscess abcès m

absolutely absolument

accelerator accélérateur m

accent accent m

accept accepter

accident accident m

accommodation logement m

account compte m

accurate exact(e)

ache douleur f

adapt adapter

adhesive tape ruban adhésif m

admission fee droit d'entrée m

adult adulte m/f

advance, in advance avance, d'avance

advertise annoncer

advertisement publicité f

advise conseiller

aeroplane avion m

afraid of (to be) avoir peur de

after après

afternoon après-midi m

afterwards après, ensuite

again encore, à nouveau

against contre

age âge m

ago, a week ago il y a, il y a une semaine

agree être d'accord

agreement accord m

air air m

air conditioning climatisation f

air ticket billet d'avion m

airmail courrier par avion m

airport aéroport m

aisle bas-côté m

aisle seat allée f, couloir m

all right d'accord

allow permettre

almond amande f

almost presque

alone seul(e)

Alps Alpes fpl

already déjà

also aussi

although bien que

altogether entièrement, tout à fait

always toujours

am, I am suis, je suis

a.m. (before noon) le matin, du matin

amazing stupéfiant, sensationnel

amber ambre m

ambulance ambulance f

among parmi

amount montant m

anaesthetic anesthésique m

ancient ancien, antique

and et

angry en colère

animal animal m

ankle cheville f

anniversary anniversaire (de mariage, etc.) m

annoy ennuyer

annual annuel

another un(e) autre

answer (vb) répondre

ant fourmi f

antacid antiacide m

anybody n'importe qui

anything n'importe quoi

apology excuse f

appendicitis appendicite f

appointment rendez-vous m

apron tablier m

are (we are, you are, they are) nous sommes, vous êtes, ils/elles sont

area endroit m, zone f

armchair fauteuil m

arrange arranger

arrest (vb) arrêter

arrival arrivée f

art art m

Atlantic Ocean Océan Atlantique m

attack (n) attaque f

attic grenier m, mansarde f

audience public m, audience f

aunt tante f

auto-teller billetterie f, distributeur automatique de billets m

autumn automne m

available disponible

avalanche avalanche f

avenue avenue f

average moyen(ne)

avoid éviter

awake réveillé(e)

away loin, parti(e)

awful terrible

B

baby food aliment pour bébés m

back dos m

backache mal de dos m

backpack sac à dos m

bacon bacon m

bad mauvais

badly mal

bag sac m

baggage bagage m

baggage claim livraison des bagages f

bait amorce f, appat m

bakery boulangerie f

balcony balcon m

ENGLISH → FRENCH

ENGLISH → FRENCH

ballpoint pen stylo bille m
bandage bandage m
bar of chocolate tablette de chocolat f
bark (vb) aboyer
barn grange f
barrel tonneau m
basement sous-sol m
basket panier m
bath bain m, baignoire f
bathroom salle de bains f
bay baie f
bay leaf laurier m
beach plage f
bean haricot m
beard barbe f
beautiful beau/belle
beauty salon institut de beauté m
because parce que, à cause de
bed lit m
bed & breakfast bed & breakfast m, chambre et petit déjeuner f
bee abeille f
beef bœuf m
before avant
beginner débutant(e)
behind derrière
believe croire
bell sonnette f, cloche f
below en bas
belt ceinture f
bend (n) virage m

bend (vb) plier, courber
beside à côté
bet (n) pari m
bet (vb) parier
better mieux, meilleur(e)
beyond au-delà
bicycle vélo m
big gros/grosse
bill compte m, addition f
bin poubelle f
binoculars jumelles fpl
bird oiseau m
birth naissance f
birth certificate acte (m) de naissance
birthday anniversaire m
birthday card carte d'anniversaire f
birthday present cadeau d'anniversaire m
biscuit biscuit m
bit bout, morceau m
bite (n) morsure (animal) f, bouchée (food) f
bite (vb) mordre
black noir(e)
black ice verglas m
blackcurrant cassis m
blanket couverture f
bleach eau de Javel f
bleed saigner
blind (adj) aveugle
blind (n) store m
blister ampoule f
block of flats immeuble m

blocked bloqué(e)

blood sang m

blood pressure tension artérielle f

blouse blouse f

blow-dry brushing

blue bleu(e)

blunt émoussé

blusher fard à joues m

boar sanglier m

boarding card carte d'embarquement f

boarding house pension f

boat bateau m

boat trip excursion en bateau f

body corps m

boil (vb) bouillir

bone os m

bonnet (car) capot m

book (n) livre m

book (vb) réserver

bookshop librairie f

boot (car) coffre m

boots bottes fpl

border frontière f

boring ennuyeux

born né(e)

borrow emprunter

both tous les deux

bottle bouteille f

bottle opener décapsuleur m

bottom (at the) au fond, en bas

bow tie nœud papillon m

bowl bol m

box boîte f

boy garçon m

boyfriend ami, copain m

bra soutien-gorge m

bracelet bracelet m

brake frein m

brake fluid liquide de freins m

brake light feu de stop m

branch branche, filiale f

brand marque f

brandy brandy m

bread pain m

break (n) pause f

break (vb) casser

breakable cassable

breakdown panne f

breakdown (nervous) dépression nerveuse f

breakfast petit déjeuner m

break-in cambriolage m

breast poitrine f, sein m

breathe respirer

breeze brise f

brewery brasserie f

bride mariée f

bridegroom marié m

bridge pont

briefcase porte-documents m

bright brillant, clair

bring apporter, amener

Britain Grande Bretagne f

ENGLISH → FRENCH

British britannique, Britannique
brochure brochure f
bronchitis bronchite f
brooch broche f
broom balai m
brother frère m
brother-in-law beau-frère m
brown marron
brown (hair) brun(e)
bruise bleu m
brush brosse f, pinceau m
Brussels Bruxelles
bucket seau m
buffet car voiture-buffet f
buggy buggy m
build construire
building bâtiment m
bulb (electric) ampoule f
bulb (plant) bulbe m
bumper pare-choc m
bun brioche f
bunch bouquet m
bureau de change bureau de change m
burglar cambrioleur m
burglary cambriolage m
burn brûler
burst éclater
bus (auto)bus m, car m
bus stop arrêt d'autobus m
bush buisson m
business affaires fpl

business trip voyage d'affaires m
busy occupé(e)
but mais
butcher boucher m
butter beurre m
butterfly papillon m
button bouton m
buy acheter
by par
bypass (medical) pontage m
bypass (road) bretelle de contournement f

C
cab taxi m
cabbage chou m
cabin cabine f
cable car téléphérique m
cake gâteau m
cake shop pâtisserie f
calculator calculette f
calf (anatomy) mollet m
calf (animal) veau m
call (n) appel m
call (vb) appeler
calm calme
camp (vb) camper
camp site terrain de camping m
can (n) boîte f
can (vb, be able to) pouvoir
can opener ouvre-boîte m

Canada Canada m
canal canal m
cancel annuler
cancellation annulation f
cancer cancer m
candle bougie f
candy bonbon m
canoe canoë m
cap casquette f
capital (city) capitale f
capital (finance) capital m
car voiture f
car ferry ferry-boat m
car parts pièces de rechange f
caravan caravane f
caravan site camping pour caravanes m
carburettor carburateur m
card carte f
cardboard carton m
cardigan cardigan m
careful prudent(e)
caretaker gardien(ne)
carpenter charpentier m
carpet tapis m
carriage wagon m
carrier bag sac (en plastique) m
carrot carotte f
carry porter
carry-cot couffin m
carton boîte en carton f

carwash lavage de voiture m
case caisse f
cash espèces f, liquide m
cash desk caisse f
cash dispenser distributeur de billets m
cashier caissier m, caissière f
cassette cassette f
castle château m
casualty department service des urgences m
cat chat m
catch attraper
cathedral cathédrale f
Catholic catholique
cauliflower chou-fleur m
cave grotte f
CD player platine laser f, lecteur de CD m
ceiling plafond m
celery céleri m
cellar cave f
cemetery cimetière m
Centigrade centigrade m
centimetre centimètre m
centre centre m
century siècle m
certain certain(e)
certainly certainement
certificate certificat m
chair chaise f

ENGLISH → FRENCH

chair lift télésiège m
chambermaid femme de chambre f
Champagne champagne m
change (n, money) monnaie f
change (vb) changer
changing room vestiaire m
Channel (English) La Manche f
channel (TV) chaîne f
chapel chapelle f
charcoal charbon de bois m
charcoal (colour) anthracite
charge prix m
charge card carte de crédit f
charter flight charter m
cheap bon marché, pas cher
cheap rate à tarif réduit
check (vb) vérifier, contrôler
check-in enregistrement m, check-in m
cheek joue f
cheers! à votre (ta) santé!
cheering réconfortant
cheese fromage m
chef chef, cuisinier m
chemist pharmacien(ne)
cheque chèque m

cheque book chéquier m
cheque card carte d'identité bancaire f
cherry (brandy) cherry m
cherry (fruit) cerise f
chess échecs m
chest poitrine f
chest of drawers commode f
chestnut châtaigne f
chewing-gum chewing-gum m
chicken poulet m
chicken pox varicelle f
child enfant m/f
child car seat siège auto pour enfants m
chimney cheminée f
chin menton m
china porcelaine f
China Chine f
Chinese chinois(e), Chinois(e)
chips frites f, chips m
chives ciboulette f
chocolate chocolat m
chocolates chocolats m
choir choeur m
choose choisir
chop (n) côtelette f
Christian name, first name prénom m
Christmas Noël m
Christmas Eve Réveillon de Noël m

church église f
cider cidre m
cigar cigare m
cigarette cigarette f
cigarette lighter
  briquet m
cinema cinéma m
circle cercle m
cistern citerne f
citizen citoyen(ne)
city centre centre-
  ville m
class classe f
clean propre
cleaning solution
  détachant m
clear claire
clever astucieux, intelligent m, astucieuse,
  intelligente f
cliff falaise f
climb (vb) grimper
cling film film
  alimentaire m
clinic clinique f
cloakroom vestiaire m
clock réveil m
close (vb) fermer
cloth chiffon m, lavette f
clothes vêtements mpl,
  habillement mpl
clothes line corde à
  linge f
clothes peg épingle à
  linge f
cloud nuage m
clutch (n) embrayage m
coach car m

coal charbon m
coast côte f
coastguard garde-
  côte m
coat manteau m
coat hanger cintre,
  porte-manteau m
cockroach cafard m
cocoa cacao m
coconut noix de coco f
cod morue f,
  cabillaud m
code code m
coffee café m
coil (n) rouleau m,
  bobine f
coin pièce f
Coke coca-cola m
colander passoire f
cold froid(e)
collapse (vb)
  s'effondrer
collar col m
collarbone clavicule f
colleague collègue m/f
collect (vb) recueillir,
  collecter
collect call appel en
  PCV m
colour couleur f
colour blind
  daltonien(ne)
colour film film en
  couleur m
comb peigne m
come venir
come back revenir
come in entrer

comedy comédie f
comfortable confortable
company compagnie f
compartment compartiment m
compass boussole f
complain se plaindre
complaint plainte f
completely complètement
composer compositeur m
compulsory obligatoire
computer ordinateur m
concert concert m
concession concession f
concussion commotion f
condition condition f
condom préservatif m
conference conférence f
confirm confirmer
confirmation confirmation f
confused désorienté(e)
congratulations félicitation f
connecting flight correspondance f
connection rapport m, correspondance f
conscious conscient(e)
constipated constipé(e)
consulate consulat m

contact (n) contact m
contact (vb) joindre
contact lenses verres de contact m
continue continuer
contraceptive contraceptif m
contract contrat m
convenient commode
cook (vb) faire cuire
cooker cuisinière f
cookie biscuit m
cooking ustensils ustensiles de cuisine mpl
cool frais, fraîche
cool bag/box sac isotherme m, glacière f
copy (n) copie f
cork bouchon m
corkscrew tire-bouchon m
corner coin m
correct juste
corridor couloir m
cost prix, coût m
cot berceau m
cotton coton m
cotton wool coton hydrophile m
couch canapé m
couchette couchette f
cough (n) toux f
cough (vb) tousser
cough mixture sirop pour la toux m
counter comptoir m
country pays m

ENGLISH → FRENCH

countryside campagne f

couple couple m, quelques

courier service messagerie f

course cours m, plat (meals) m

cousin cousin(e) m/f

cover charge couvert m

cow vache f

crab crabe m

craft artisanat m

cramp crampe f

crash collision f

crash helmet casque de protection m

cream crème f

crèche crèche f

credit card carte de crédit f

crime crime m

crisps chips

crockery vaisselle f

cross (n) croix f

cross (vb) traverser

crossing croisement m

crossroads carrefour m

crossword puzzle mots croisés m

crowd foule f

crowded encombré(e), plein(e) de monde

crown couronne f

cruise croisière f

crutches béquilles f

cry (n) cri m

cry (vb) pleurer, crier

crystal cristal m

cucumber concombre m

cufflinks boutons de manchettes m

cup tasse f, coupe f

cupboard placard m

curly bouclé(e)

currency devise f

current courant m

curtain rideau m

cushion coussin m

custard crème anglaise f

custom coutume f

customer client(e) m/f

customs douane f

cut (vb) couper

cutlery couverts m

cycle cycle m

cycle track piste cyclable f

cyst kyste m

cystitis cystite f

Czech Republic République Tchèque f

D

daily quotidien(ne), tous les jours

damage dommages m, dégâts m

damp humide

dance danse f

danger danger m

ENGLISH → FRENCH

ENGLISH → FRENCH

dangerous dangereux/
   dangereuse
dark sombre
date date f
date of birth date de
   naissance f
dates dates f
daughter fille f
daughter-in-law belle-
   fille f
dawn aube f
day jour m
dead mort(e)
deaf sourd(e)
deal marché m
dear cher/chère
death mort f
debts dettes fpl
decaffeinated
   décaféiné
December décembre
decide décider
decision décision f
deck chair chaise
   longue f
deduct déduire
deep profond(e)
definitely certainement
degree degré m
delay (n) délai m
deliberately délibérément
delicious délicieux/
   délicieuse
deliver livrer
Denmark Danemark m
dental floss fil
   dentaire m

dentist dentiste m
dentures dentier m
depart partir
department service,
   département, rayon m
department store
   grand magasin m
departure départ m
departure lounge salle
   d'embarquement f
deposit acompte m,
   arrhes f
describe décrire
description
   description f
desk bureau m
dessert dessert m
destination
   destination f
details détails m,
   coordonnées fpl
detergent détergent m
detour détour m
develop développer
diabetic diabétique
dial (vb) composer
dialling code indicatif m
dialling tone tonalité f
diamond diamant
diaper couche f
diarrhoea diarrhée f
diary agenda m
dice dé m
dictionary dictionnaire m
die (vb) mourir
diesel diesel m
diet régime m
difference différence f

different différent(e)
difficult difficile
dinghy youyou, canot m
dining room salle à manger f
dinner dîner m
direct (adj) direct(e)
direction direction f
directory (phone) annuaire m
dirty sale
disabled handicapé(e)
disappear disparaître
disappointed déçu(e)
disaster catastrophe f
disconnected coupé(e)
discount (n) rabais m
discover découvrir
disease maladie f
dish plat m
dishtowel torchon m
dishwasher lave-vaisselle m
disinfectant désinfectant m
disk disque m
disposable nappies couches à jeter fpl
distance distance f
district quartier m
disturb déranger
dive (vb) plonger
diving board tremplin m
divorced divorcé(e)
DIY shop magasin de bricolage m
dizzy pris(e) de vertiges

do ... ? est-ce que ... ?
do (vb) faire
doctor médecin m
document document m
dog chien m
doll poupée f
domestic domestique m/f
door porte f
doorbell sonnette f
doorman portier m
double double
double bed lit à deux places m
double room chambre pour deux personnes f
doughnut beignet m
downhill en pente
downstairs en bas
dozen douzaine f
drain (n) canalisation f
draught courant d'air m
draught beer bière à la pression f
drawer tiroir m
drawing dessin m
dreadful terrible
dress (n) robe f
dressing (salad) assaisonnement m
dressing gown robe de chambre f
drill (n) perceuse f
drink (n) boisson f
drink (vb) boire
drinking water eau potable f
drive (vb) conduire

ENGLISH → FRENCH

99

driver chauffeur m
driving licence permis de conduire m
drop (n) goutte f
drop (vb) laisser tomber
drug (n) drogue f
drunk ivre, soûl(e)
dry sec/sèche
dry cleaner's teinturier m, pressing m
dryer séchoir m
duck canard m
due somme due f
dull terne
dummy mannequin m
during pendant
dust (n) poussière f
dustbin poubelle f
duster plumeau m
dustpan pelle f
Dutch hollandais(e), Hollandais(e)
duty-free hors taxes
duvet couette f
duvet cover housse de couette f
dye (n) teinture f
dynamo dynamo f

E
each chaque
eagle aigle m
ear oreille f
earache mal d'oreilles m, otite f
earphones écouteurs m

earrings boucles d'oreilles f
earth terre f
earthquake tremblement de terre m
east est
Easter, Happy Easter! Pâques, Joyeuses Pâques!
easy facile
eat manger
EC CE f
economy économie f
economy class classe économie f
edge bord m
eel anguille f
egg œuf m
either ... or ou ... ou, soit ... soit
elastic band élastique m
elbow coude m
electric électrique
electrician électricien m
electricity électricité f
elevator ascenseur m
embassy ambassade f
emergency urgence f
emergency exit sortie de secours f
empty vide
end fin f
engaged occupé(e)
engaged (to be married) fiancé(e)
engine moteur m
engineer ingénieur m
England Angleterre f

English anglais(e)
Englishman/woman Anglais(e)
enjoy s'amuser (fun), serégaler (food)
enlargement agrandissement **m**
enough assez
enquiry demande de renseignements, enquête **f**
enquiry desk bureau des renseignements **m**
enter entrer
entrance entrée **f**
entrance fee droit d'entrée **m**
envelope enveloppe **f**
epileptic épileptique
equipment équipement **m**
error erreur **f**
escalator escalier roulant, escalator **m**
escape (vb) s'échapper
especially spéciale-ment
essential essentiel(le)
estate agent agent immobilier
Estonia Estonie **f**
EU EU **f**
Europe Europe **f**
European européen(ne)
even même
evening soir **m**, soirée **f**

eventually finalement
everyone chacun(e)
everything tout
everywhere partout
exactly exactement
examination examen **m**
example, for example exemple **m**, par exemple
excellent excellent(e)
except excepté, sauf
excess luggage excédent de bagages **m**
exchange échange **m**
exciting excitant(e), passionnant(e)
exclude exclure
excursion excursion **f**
excuse me excusez-moi
exhaust pipe pot d'échappement **m**
exhausted épuisé(e)
exhibition exposition **f**
exit sortie **f**
expect attendre, s'attendre à
expenses dépenses **f**
expensive cher/chère
experienced expérimenté(e)
expire expirer
explain expliquer
explosion explosion **f**
export (n) exportation **f**
export (vb) exporter

ENGLISH → FRENCH

ENGLISH → FRENCH

exposure (photo)
pose f
express (vb) exprimer
express (post) exprès
extra supplémentaire
extraordinary extra-
ordinaire
eye, eyes œil, yeux m
eye drops gouttes pour
les yeux f
eye make-up remover
démaquillant pour les
yeux m
eye shadow ombre à
paupières f

F
face visage m
factory usine f
faint (vb) s'évanouir
fair (hair colour)
blond(e)
fair (just) juste
fairly assez,
équitablement
fake faux m
fall (n) chute f
fall (vb) tomber
false faux/fausse
family famille f
famous célèbre
fan (n) éventail m,
ventilateur m
fan belt courroie de
ventilateur f
far loin
fare tarif m
farm ferme f

farmer fermier m,
fermière f
farmhouse maison de
ferme f
fashionable à la mode
fast rapide
fasten attacher
fasten seat belt
attachez votre ceinture
fat gros(se)
father père m
father-in-law beau-
père m
fatty gras(se)
fault faute f, défaut m
faulty défectueux,
défectueuse
favourite préféré(e),
favori/favorite
fax télécopie f, fax m
February février
feed nourrir
feel sentir
feet pieds m
female (animal)
femelle f
female (gender)
féminin
fence barrière f
fender pare-feu m
ferry ferry-boat m
festival festival m
fetch aller chercher
fever fièvre f,
température f
few, a few peu,
quelques
fiancé fiancé m

fiancée fiancée f
field champ m
fight (n) bataille f
fight (vb) se battre
file (n) dossier m
fill, fill in remplir
fill up (petrol) faites le plein
fillet filet m
filling (sandwich) garniture f
filling (tooth) plombage m
film film m
film processing développement de photos
filter filtre m
filthy dégoûtant(e)
find (vb) trouver
fine! parfait!
finger doigt m
finish (vb) finir
fire feu m
fire brigade pompiers mpl
fire exit sortie de secours
fire extinguisher extincteur m
first premier/première
first, at first d'abord, premièrement
first aid secours d'urgence m
first-aid kit trousse à pharmacie f

first class première classe f
first floor premier étage m
first name prénom m
fish poisson m
fishing permit permis de pêche m
fishing rod canne à pêche f
fishmonger poissonnier m
fit en forme (health), adapté(e)
fitting room salon d'essayage m
fix (vb) réparer, fixer
fizzy pétillant(e)
flag drapeau m
flannel flanelle f
flash flash m
flashlight torche électrique f
flask bouteille f, thermos f
flat (adj) plat(e)
flat (n) appartement m
flat battery, flat tyre batterie à plat, pneu à plat
flavour goût m, parfum m
flaw défaut m
flea puce f
flea market marché aux puces m
flight vol m

ENGLISH → FRENCH

flip flops tongs f, sandales de plage f
flippers palmes f
flood inondation f
floor sol m, étage m
floorcloth serpillière f
florist fleuriste m/f
flour farine f
flower fleur f
flu grippe f
fluent coulant(e)
fluently couramment
fly (n) mouche f
fly (vb) voler (bird), prendre l'avion
fog brouillard m
folk gens m
follow suivre
food nourriture f, alimentation f
food poisoning intoxication alimentaire f
food shop magasin d'alimentation m
foot pied m
football, football match football m, match de football m
footpath passage m, sentier m
for pour
forbidden interdit(e)
foreign, foreigner étranger m, étrangère f
forest forêt f
forget oublier
fork fourchette f
form formulaire m

formal formel(le)
fortnight quinzaine de jours f
fortress forteresse f
fortunately heureusement
fountain fontaine f
four-wheel drive à quatre roues motrices, quatre-quatre f
fox renard m
fracture fracture f
frame cadre m
France France f
free libre, gratuit(e)
freelance indépendant(e), free-lance m
freeway autoroute f
freezer congélateur m
French français(e)
Frenchman/woman Français(e)
frequent fréquent(e)
fresh frais m, fraîche f
Friday vendredi m
fridge réfrigérateur, frigo m
fried frit(e)
friend ami(e)
friendly amical(e)
frog grenouille f
from de, de la part de
front (in ... of) devant
frost gelée f
frozen gelé(e), surgelé(e) (food)
fruit fruit m
fruit juice jus de fruit m

fruitcake cake m
fry frire
frying pan poêle f
fuel carburant m
fuel gauge jauge de carburant f
full plein(e)
full board pension complète f
fun amusement m
funeral obsèques f
funicular funiculaire m
funny amusant(e)
fur fourrure f
fur coat manteau de fourrure m
furnished meublé(e)
furniture meuble m
further davantage, plus loin
fuse fusible m
fuse box boîte à fusibles f
future (tense) futur m
future (time) avenir m

G

gallery galerie f
gallon gallon m
game (animal) gibier m
game (play) jeu m
garage garage m
garden jardin m
garlic ail m
gas gaz m
gas cylinder bouteille de gaz f

gas cooker cuisinière à gaz f, gazinière f
gate barrière, porte f
gay homosexuel/ homosexuelle
gay bar bar pour homosexuels m
gear équipement m
gear lever levier de changement de vitesse m
gearbox boîte de vitesses f
general général(e)
generous généreux/ généreuse
Geneva Genève
gents' toilet hommes
genuine authentique
German allemand(e), Allemand(e)
German measles rubéole f
Germany Allemagne f
get devenir, avoir, obtenir
get on, get off monter, descendre
gift cadeau m
girl fille f
girlfriend amie f
give donner
give back rendre
glacier glacier m
glad content(e)
glass verre m
glasses (spectacles) lunettes f
gloves gants m

ENGLISH → FRENCH

glue colle f
go aller
go away partir
go back retourner
goat chèvre f
God Dieu m
goggles lunettes
  protectrices f, masque
  de plongée m
gold or m
golf club club de golfe m
golf course terrain de
  golf m
good bon/bonne
**good afternoon, good
  day** bonjour
good evening bonsoir
Good Friday Vendredi
  Saint m
good morning bonjour
good night bonne nuit
goodbye au revoir
goose oie f
Gothic gothique
government gouverne-
  ment m
gradually graduelle-
  ment
gram gramme m
grammar grammaire f
grand magnifique,
  grandiose
granddaughter petite-
  fille f
grandfather grand-
  père m
grandmother grand-
  mère f

grandparents grands-
  parents m
grandson petit-fils m
grape raisin m
grass herbe f
grated râpé(e)
grateful
  reconnaissant(e)
gravy jus de viande m
greasy gras/grasse
great merveilleux/
  merveilleuse, formidable
Great Britain Grande-
  Bretagne f
Greece Grèce f
Greek grec/grecque,
  Grec/Grecque
green vert(e)
greengrocer épicier m
greeting salutations fpl
grey gris(e)
grilled grillé(e)
ground sol m
ground floor rez-de-
  chaussée m
group groupe m
guarantee garantie f
guard garde f
guest invité(e) m/f
guesthouse pension f
guide guide m
guidebook guide
  touristique m
guided tour voyage
  organisé m
guitar guitare f
gun fusil m
gym gymnastique f

H

hail grêle f

hair cheveux m

hairbrush brosse à cheveux f

haircut coupe de cheveux f

hairdresser coiffeur m, coiffeuse f

hairdryer séchoir à cheveux m

half moitié f, demie f

hall hall m

ham jambon m

hamburger hamburger m

hammer marteau m

hand main f

handbag sac à main m

handbrake frein à main m

handicapped handicapé(e)

handkerchief mouchoir m

handle poignée f, manche m

handmade fait à la main

handsome beau

hang up (telephone) raccrocher

hanger cintre, porte-manteau m

hang-gliding delta-plane m

hangover gueule de bois f

happen arriver, se passer

happy heureux/heureuse

harbour port m

hard dur(e)

hard disk disque dur m

hardly à peine

hardware shop quincaillerie m

hare lièvre m

harvest cueillette, moisson f

hat chapeau m

have avoir

hay fever rhume des foins m

hazelnut noisette f

he il

head tête f

headache mal de tête m

headlights phares mpl

headphones écouteurs m

health food shop magasin de produits diététiques m

healthy sain(e), bien portant(e)

hear entendre

hearing aid appareil acoustique m

heart cœur m

heart attack crise cardiaque f

heartburn brûlure d'estomac f

ENGLISH → FRENCH

ENGLISH → FRENCH

heat chaleur f
heater appareil de chauffage f, chauffe-eau (water heater) m
heating chauffage m
heavy lourd(e)
heel talon m
height hauteur f
helicopter hélicoptère m
helmet casque m
Help! Au secours!
help (vb) aider
hem ourlet m
her, to her la, lui
her (possessive) son, sa, ses
herbal tea tisane f
herbs fines herbes f
here ici
hernia hernie f
hide (vb) cacher
high haut(e)
high blood pressure hypertension f
high chair chaise haute pour enfants f
high tide marée haute f
him le, lui
hip hanche f
hip replacement pose d'une prothèse de la hanche f
hire (vb) louer
hire car voiture de location f
his son, sa, ses
historic historique

history histoire f
hit (vb) cogner
hitchhike faire du stop
hold (vb) tenir, contenir
hole trou m
holiday vacances fpl, congé m
holy saint(e)
home maison f, foyer m
homesickness nostalgie f, mal du pays m
honest honnête
honey miel m
honeymoon lune de miel f
hood capuchon m
hope espérance f, espoir m
hopefully avec un peu d'espoir
horn corne (animal) f, avertisseur (car) m
horse cheval m
horse racing course de chevaux f
horse riding équitation f
hose pipe tuyau d'arrosage m
hospital hôpital m
hospitality hospitalité f
hostel foyer m, auberge f
hot chaud(e)
hot spring source chaude f

hot-water bottle
  bouillotte f
hour heure f
hourly toutes les
  heures
house maison f
house wine cuvée du
  patron f
housework ménage m
hovercraft aéro-
  glisseur m
how? comment?
how are you?
  comment allez-vous?
  (formal), ça va?
  (informal)
how do you do?
  bonjour, enchanté(e)
  (formal)
how many? combien?
how much is it? c'est
  combien?
humid humide
humour humour m
Hungarian hongrois(e),
  Hongrois(e)
Hungary Hongrie f
hungry (to be) avoir
  faim
hunt (n) chasse f
hunting permit permis
  de chasse m
husband mari m
hydrofoil hydrofoil m
hypodermic needle
  aiguille hypodermique f

I
I je
ice glace f
ice cream glace f
ice rink patinoire f
ice skates patins à
  glace m
iced coffee café
  glacé m
idea idée f
identity card carte
  d'identité f
if si
ignition allumage m
ignition key clé de
  contact f
ill malade
illness maladie f
immediately
  immédiatement
important important(e)
impossible impossible
improve améliorer
in en, dans
inch pouce
included compris(e),
  inclus(e)
inconvenient gênant(e)
incredible incroyable
Indian indien/indienne,
  Indien/Indienne
indicator indicateur m,
  clignotant m
indigestion
  indigestion f
indoor pool piscine
  couverte f
indoors à l'intérieur

ENGLISH → FRENCH

infection infection f
infectuous contagieux/contagieuse
inflammation inflammation f
informal simple, sans façon
information renseignement m, information f
ingredient ingrédient m
injection injection f, piqûre f
injured blessé(e)
injury blessure f
ink encre f
in-laws beaux-parents m
inn auberge f
inner tube chambre à air f
insect insecte m
insect bite piqûre d'insecte f
insect repellent produit insectifuge m
inside à l'intérieur
insist insister
insomnia insomnie f
instant coffee café instantané m
instead au lieu de
insulin insuline f
insurance assurance f
intelligent intelligent(e)
interesting intéressant(e)
international international(e)

interpreter interprète m/f
intersection intersection f
interval intervalle m
into en, dans
introduce introduire
invitation invitation f
invite (vb) inviter
invoice facture f
Ireland Irlande f
Irish irlandais(e)
Irishman/woman Irlandais(e)
iron (n) fer m, fer à repasser m
ironing board planche à repasser f
ironmonger's quincaillerie f
is est
island île f
it, it is il, elle, ce, c'est
Italian italien/italienne, Italien/Italienne
Italy Italie f
itch démangeaison f

J
jack cric m
jacket veste f
jam confiture f
jammed coincé(e)
January janvier
jar bocal m
jaundice jaunisse f
jaw mâchoire f
jealous jaloux/jalouse

jellyfish méduse **f**
jersey jersey **m**
Jew/Jewess Juif/Juive
jeweller bijoutier **m**, joaillier **m**
jewellery bijouterie **f**
Jewish juif/juive
job travail **m**, boulot **m**
jog faire du jogging
join joindre, s'inscrire à (club)
joint articulation **f**
joke (vb) plaisanter
journey voyage **m**
joy joie **f**
judge (n) juge **m**
jug pichet **m**
juice jus **m**
July juillet
jump (vb) sauter
jump leads câbles de démarrage **m**
jumper pull **m**
junction jonction **f**
June juin
just juste

K
keep (vb) garder
Keep the change! Gardez la monnaie!
kettle bouilloire **f**
key clé **f**
key ring porte-clé **m**
kick (vb) donner un coup de pied
kidney rein (organ) **m**, rognon (food) **m**

kill (vb) tuer
kilo, kilogram kilo, kilogramme **m**
kilometre kilomètre **m**
kind gentil/gentille
king roi **m**
kiosk kiosque **m**
kiss (n) baiser **m**, bise **f**
kiss (vb) embrasser
kitchen cuisine **f**
kitchenette kitchenette **f**
knee genou **m**
knickers culotte **f**, slip **m**
knife couteau **m**
knit tricoter
knitting needle aiguille à tricoter **f**
knitwear lainage **m**
knock (vb) frapper
knock down démolir
knock over renverser
know savoir (something), connaître (somebody)

L
label étiquette **f**
lace dentelle **f**
lace (shoe) lacet **m**
ladder échelle
ladies' toilet dames
ladies' wear vêtements pour femmes **mpl**
lady dame **f**
lager bière blonde **f**

ENGLISH → FRENCH

lake lac m
lamb agneau m
lamp lampe f
land terre f, pays m
landlord, landlady propriétaire m/f
landslide glissement de terrain m
lane allée f
language langue f
language course cours de langue m
large grand(e)
last dernier/dernière
last night hier soir
late tard, en retard
later plus tard
Latin Quarter Quartier Latin m
laugh (vb) rire
launderette, laundromat laverie automatique f
laundry linge à laver
lavatory toilettes f
law loi f
lawyer homme de loi m, juriste m/f
laxative laxatif m
lazy paresseux/ paresseuse
lead (n) plomb m
lead (vb) mener
lead-free sans plomb
leaflet prospectus m
leak (n) fuite f
learn apprendre
lease bail m

leather cuir m
leave (vb) partir, quitter
leek poireau m
left gauche
left-handed gaucher/ gauchère
leg jambe f
lemon citron m
lemonade limonade f
lend prêter
lens lentille f, verre m
lentils lentilles f
lesbian lesbienne f
less moins
lesson leçon f
let louer
let off laisser partir
letter lettre f
letterbox boîte à lettres f
lettuce laitue f
level crossing passage à niveau m
lever levier m
library bibliothèque f
licence licence f, permis m
lid couvercle m
lie mentir
lie down s'allonger
life vie f
life insurance assurance vie f
lifebelt bouée de sauvetage f
lifeguard maître- nageur m

lifejacket gilet de sauvetage m
lift (n, elevator) ascenseur m
lift (vb) lever, soulever
light lumière f
light (adj) léger/légère
lightbulb ampoule électrique f
lightning éclair m
like (adj) comme
like (vb) aimer
lime citron vert m
line ligne f
linen linge m
lingerie lingerie f
lion lion m
lipstick rouge à lèvres m
liqueur liqueur f
list liste f
listen écouter
litre litre m
litter (n) ordures f
little petit(e), peu
live (vb) vivre
lively vivant(e)
liver foie m
liver pâté pâté de foie
living room séjour m, living-room m
loaf pain m de mie
lobby foyer m
lobster homard m
local local m
lock (n) serrure f
lock (vb) fermer à clé
lock in enfermer

locker casier m
lollipop sucette f
long (adj) long/longue
long-distance call appel longue distance m
look after s'occuper de, soigner
look at regarder
look for chercher
look forward to se réjouir à l'idée de
loose lâche
lorry camion m
lose perdre
lost perdu(e)
lost property objets trouvés mpl
lot (adv) beaucoup
lot (n) lot m
loud fort, bruyant(e)
lounge salon m
love (n) amour m
love (vb) aimer
lovely joli(e)
low bas/basse
low fat allégé(e), écrémé(e)
low tide marée basse f
luck, good luck chance f, bonne chance
lucky (to be) avoir de la chance
luggage bagage m
luggage rack porte-bagages m

ENGLISH → FRENCH

luggage tag étiquette à bagages f
luggage trolley chariot à bagages m
lump grosseur f
lunch déjeuner m
luxury luxe m

M

machine machine f
mad fou/folle
made fait
magazine magazine m
maggot ver m, asticot m
magnet aimant m
magnifying glass loupe f
maid domestique f
maiden name nom de jeune fille m
mail courrier m
main principal(e)
main course plat principal m
main post office poste centrale f
main road rue principale f
mains switch interrupteur général m
make (n) fabrication f
make (vb) faire
male (adj) masculin
male (n) mâle m
man homme m
man-made fibre synthétique m

manager directeur m, manager m
manual (n) manuel m
many beaucoup (de)
map carte f, plan m
marble marbre m
March mars
market marché m
marmalade marmelade f
married marié(e)
marsh marais m
mascara mascara m
mashed potatoes purée de pommes de terre f
Mass (religious) messe f
mast mât m
match match m
matches allumettes fpl
material tissu m, matériel m
matter matière f
matter, it doesn't matter c'est sans importance
matter, what's the matter? qu'est-ce qu'il y a?
mattress matelas m
May mai
may (vb) pouvoir
maybe peut-être
mayonnaise mayonnaise f
me moi, me
meal repas m

mean (vb) signifier
measles rougeole m
measure (vb) mesurer
meat viande f
mechanic mécanique f
medical insurance
assurance médicale f
medicine médica-
ment m
medieval médiéval(e)
Mediterranean Sea
Méditerranée f
medium moyen m,
milieu m
medium dry (wine)
demi-sec
medium rare (meat)
à point
medium sized de taille
moyenne
meet rencontrer
meeting rencontre f,
réunion f
melon melon m
melt fondre
men hommes mpl
mend réparer
meningitis méningite f
menswear vêtements
pour hommes mpl
mention (vb)
mentionner
menu menu m
meringue meringue f
message message m
metal métal m
meter mètre m
metro métro m

microwave (oven)
four à micro-ondes m
midday midi
middle milieu m
midnight minuit
might (vb) pouvoir
migraine migraine f
mile mile m
milk lait m
minced meat viande
hachée f
mind esprit m
minute (n) minute f
mirror miroir m
Miss Mademoiselle, Mlle
miss (vb) manquer
mist brume f
mistake erreur f, faute f
misunderstanding
malentendu m
mix (vb) mélanger
mix-up confusion f
mobile phone télé-
phone mobile m
moisturiser crème
hydratante f
moment moment m
monastery
monastère m
Monday lundi
money argent m
money belt ceinture-
portefeuille f
money order mandat-
poste m
month mois m
monthly mensuel/
mensuelle

ENGLISH → FRENCH

monument monument **m**
moon lune **f**
mooring mouillage **m**
more plus
morning, this morning matin **m**, ce matin
mosque mosquée **f**
mosquito moustique **m**
most le plus
mostly surtout
moth mite **f**
mother mère **f**
mother-in-law belle-mère **f**
motor moteur **m**
motorbike moto **f**
motorboat canot automobile **m**
motorway autoroute **f**
mountain montagne **f**
mountain rescue sauvetage en montagne **m**
mountaineering alpinisme **m**
mouse souris **f**
moustache moustache **f**
mouth bouche **f**
mouth ulcer aphte **m**
mouthwash bain de bouche **m**
move (vb) bouger, déménager
Mr Monsieur, M.
Mrs Madame, Mme
much beaucoup

mud boue **f**
mug chope **f**
mugged agressé(e)
mumps oreillons **mpl**
muscle muscle **m**
museum musée **m**
mushroom champignon **m**
musician musicien/musicienne
Muslim Musulman(e)
mussels moules **fpl**
must devoir
mustard moutarde **f**
mutton mouton **m**
my mon, ma, mes
myself moi-même

N
nail ongle **m**
nail brush brosse à ongles **f**
nail file lime à ongles **f**
nail polish remover dissolvant **m**
nail scissors ciseaux à ongles **m**
nail varnish/polish vernis à ongles **m**
name nom **m**
nanny bonne d'enfants **f**, nounou **f**
napkin serviette (de table)
nappy couche **f**
narrow étroit(e)
nasty désagréable, méchant(e)

national national(e)
nationality nationalité f
natural naturel/naturelle
nature nature f
nature reserve
réserve naturelle f
nausea nausée f
navy marine f
near près, proche
nearby tout près
necessary nécessaire
neck cou m
necklace collier m
need (n) besoin m
need (vb) avoir besoin
needle aiguille f
negative négatif/
négative
neighbour voisin/
voisine
neither ... nor ni ... ni
nephew neveu m
nest nid m
net filet m
Netherlands Pays-
Bas mpl
never jamais
new nouveau/nouvelle
new (brand) neuf/
neuve
New Year Nouvel An m
Happy New Year!
Bonne Année!
New Year's Eve Saint-
Sylvestre f
New Zealand Nouvelle-
Zélande f

New Zealander néo-
zélandais(e), Néo-
Zélandais (e)
news nouvelles f,
journal télévisé m
newspaper journal m
newsstand kiosque
à journaux m
next suivant(e), ensuite
nice agréable, gentil/
gentille
niece nièce f
night, last night nuit f,
hier soir
nightdress chemise
de nuit f
no non
nobody personne
noise bruit m
noisy bruyant(e)
non-alcoholic sans
alcool
non-smoking non-
fumeurs
none aucun(e)
noon midi
north nord m
Northern Ireland
Irlande du Nord f
North Sea Mer du
Nord f
Norway Norvège f
Norwegian norvégien/
norvégienne,
Norvégien/Norvégienne
nose nez m
not ne ... pas
note (n) note f

ENGLISH → FRENCH

note (vb) noter
notebook/paper carnet m, bloc-note m
nothing rien
nothing else c'est tout, rien d'autre
notice board panneau d'affichage m
novel roman m
November novembre
now maintenant
nudist beach plage de nudistes f
number nombre m
number plate numéro d'immatriculation m, plaque minéralogique f
nurse, male nurse infirmière f, infirmier m
nursery nursery f, pépinière (plants) f
nursery school école maternelle f
nursery slope piste pour débutants f
nut noix f
nut (for bolt) écrou m

O

oak chêne m
oar rame f
oats avoine f
obtain devenir, avoir, obtenir
occasionally parfois, de temps en temps
occupation occupation f

occupied (e.g. toilet) occupé
ocean océan m
October octobre
odd impair (number), bizarre
of de
off absent(e), éteint(e) (switch), avarié(e) (food)
office bureau m
often souvent
oil huile f
ointment pommade f
OK d'accord
old vieux/vieille
old-age pensioner retraité(e)
old-fashioned démodé(e)
olive olive f
olive oil huile d'olive f
omelette omelette f
on sur
once une fois
one un(e)
one-way street rue à sens unique f
onion oignon m
only seulement
open (adj) ouvert(e)
open (vb) ouvrir
open ticket billet open m
opening times heures d'ouverture fpl
opera opéra m
operation opération f

operator (phone)
opérateur/opératrice
opposite en face
optician opticien/
opticienne
or ou
orange orange f
orange juice jus
d'orange m
orchestra orchestre m
order (n) commande f
order (vb) commander
organic (vegetables)
bio(logique)
other autre
otherwise autrement
our notre, nos
out dehors, sorti(e)
out of order en panne
outdoors en plein air
outside dehors,
à l'extérieur
oven four m
ovenproof allant au four
over dessus, terminé(e)
over here, over there
par ici, par là
overcharged payer
trop cher
overcoat manteau m,
pardessus m
overdone exagéré(e),
trop cuit (food)
overheat surchauffer
overnight (vb, to stay)
passer la nuit
overtake dépasser
owe devoir

owl hibou m
owner propriétaire m/f

P
pacemaker stimulateur
cardiaque m, pace-
maker m
pack (vb) emballer
package paquet m
package holiday
voyage organisé m
packet colis m
padlock cadenas m
page page f
paid payé(e)
pail seau m
pain douleur f
painful douloureux
painkiller calmant m,
analgésique m
paint (vb) peindre
painting peinture f
pair paire f
palace palais m,
palace m
pale pâle
pan casserole f
pancake crêpe f
panties slip m
pants pantalon m
pantyhose collant m
paper papier m
paper napkin serviette
en papier f
parcel colis m
pardon? pardon?
parents parents m

ENGLISH → FRENCH

parents-in-law beaux-parents **mpl**
park parc **m**
parking disk disque de stationnement **m**
parking meter parc-mètre **m**
parking ticket contravention **f**
part partie **f**
partner (friend) compagnon **m**, compagne **f**
partner (game) partenaire **m/f**
party (celebration) fête **f**, soirée **f**
party (political) parti **m**
pass (n) laissez-passer **m**
pass (vb) passer
pass control contrôle des laissez-passer **m**
passenger passager/passagère
passport passeport **m**
past passé(e)
pastry pâtisserie **f**
pastry shop pâtisserie **f**
path chemin **m**, sentier **m**
patient patient(e)
pattern motif **m**, modèle **m**
pavement trottoir **m**
payphone téléphone public **m**

peach pêche **f**
peak pic **m**
peak rate plein tarif **m**
peanut cacahuète **f**
pear poire **f**
pearl perle **f**
peas petit pois **mpl**
peculiar étrange, bizarre
pedal pédale **f**
pedestrian piéton **m**
pedestrian crossing passage pour piétons **m**
peel (vb) peler, éplucher
peg pince à linge (washing) **f**, piquet (tent) **m**
pen stylo **m**
pencil crayon **m**
penfriend correspondant(e)
peninsula péninsule **f**
people peuple **m**, gens **m**
pepper (spice) poivre **m**
pepper (vegetable) poivron **m**
per par
perfect parfait(e)
performance représentation (theatre) **f**, performance **f**
perfume parfum **m**
perhaps peut-être
period période **f**, règles (menstruation) **fpl**
perm permanente **f**

permit permis m

person personne f

pet animal familier m

petrol essence f, pétrole m

petrol can bidon d'essence

petrol station station-service f

pharmacy pharmacie f

phone téléphone m

phone book annuaire m

phone booth cabine téléphonique f

phone call appel téléphonique m

phone card télécarte f

phone number numéro de téléphone m

photo, to take a photo photo f, prendre une photo

photocopy photocopie f

phrase book guide de conversation m

piano piano m

pickpocket pickpocket m

picnic pique-nique m

picture image f

picture frame cadre à photo m

pie tourte f

piece pièce f

pig cochon m

pill pilule f

pillow oreiller m

pillowcase taie d'oreiller f

pilot pilote m

pin épingle f

pineapple ananas m

pink rose

pipe pipe f

pity (n) pitié f

pity (vb) avoir pitié de

place place f

plain simple

plait natte f, tresse f

plane avion m

plant plante f

plaster (building) plâtre m

plaster (sticking) sparadrap m

plastic plastique m

plate assiette f

platform plate-forme f

play (n) pièce (theatre) f

play (vb) jouer

playground aire de jeux f

please s'il vous plaît

pleased satisfait(e)

pleased to meet you enchanté(e)

plenty en grande quantité

pliers pinces fpl

plug bonde (sink) f, prise (electrical) f

plum prune f

plumber plombier m

ENGLISH → FRENCH

121

p.m. de l'après-midi, du soir
poached poché(e)
pocket poche f
point pointe f
points points m
poison poison m
poisonous vénéneux/ vénéneuse, toxique
Poland Pologne f
police police f
police station commissariat de police m, gendarmerie f
policeman policier m, agent de police m/f
Polish, Pole polonais(e), Polonais(e)
polish (vb) polir
polite poli(e)
polluted pollué(e)
pool bassin m
poor pauvre
poppy coquelicot m
popular populaire
population population f
pork porc m
port (harbour) port m
port (wine) porto m
porter porteur m
portion portion f
portrait portrait m
Portugal Portugal m
Portuguese portugais(e), Portugais(e)
posh chic m/f
possible possible

post poste m, Poste f
post box boîte postale f
post office bureau de poste m
postage tarif postal m
postage stamp timbre-poste m
postal code code postal m
postcard carte postale f
poster affiche f, poster m
postman facteur m
postpone renvoyer à plus tard
potato pomme de terre f
pothole fondrière f
pottery poterie f
pound livre f
pour verser
powder poudre f
powdered milk lait en poudre m
power cut panne d'électricité f
practice pratique f, entraînement m
practise pratiquer
pram voiture d'enfant f, landau m
prawn crevette f
pray prier
prefer préférer
pregnant enceinte

ENGLISH → FRENCH

prescription
ordonnance f
present (adj) présent(e)
present (n) cadeau m
present (vb) présenter
pressure pression f
pretty joli(e)
price prix m
priest prêtre m
prime minister premier
ministre m
print (vb) imprimer,
développer (photo)
printed matter
imprimés m
prison prison f
private privé(e)
prize prix
probably probablement
problem problème m
programme, program
programme m
prohibited interdit(e),
défendu(e)
promise (n) promesse f
promise (vb) promettre
pronounce prononcer
properly correctement
Protestant protestant(e)
public public/publique
public holiday jour
férié m
pudding dessert m
pull tirer
pullover pull m,
pull-over m
pump (n) pompe f
pump (vb) pomper

puncture crevaison f
puppet show
spectacle de
marionnettes m
purple violet/violette
purse porte-monnaie m
push pousser
pushchair poussette f
put ... up dresser
pyjamas pyjama m
Pyrenees Pyrénées fpl

Q
quality qualité f
quantity quantité f
quarantine
quarantaine f
quarrel dispute f
quarter (fraction)
quart m
quarter (part of town)
quartier m
quay quai m
queen reine f
question question f
queue (n) queue f
queue (vb) faire la
queue
quickly vite
quiet tranquille
quite tout à fait

R
rabbit lapin m
rabies rage f
race course f, race f
racecourse champ
de course m

123

ENGLISH → FRENCH

racket raquette f
radiator radiateur m
radio radio f
radish radis m
rag chiffon m, lavette f
railway chemin de fer m
railway station gare f
rain, it is raining
pluie f, il pleut
raincoat
imperméable m
raisin raisin sec m
rake râteau m
rape viol m
rare (meat) saignant(e)
rare (seldom) rare
rash éruption f
raspberry framboise f
rat rat m
rate (of exchange)
taux (de change) m
raw cru(e)
razor rasoir m
razor blades lames
de rasoir fpl
read lire
ready prêt(e)
real vrai(e), réel/réelle
realize se rendre
compte, comprendre
really vraiment
rearview mirror
rétroviseur m
reasonable raisonnable
receipt reçu m
receiver receveur m,
combiné (phone)
recently récemment

reception réception f
receptionist
réceptionniste m/f
recharge recharger
recipe recette f
recognize reconnaître
recommend
recommander
record (n) disque
(music) m, dossier
(legal) m
red rouge
red wine vin rouge m
redcurrants groseilles
rouges f
reduce réduire
reduction réduction f
refund (vb) rembourser
refuse (n) déchets m
refuse (vb) refuser
region région f
register (n) registre m
register (vb) s'inscrire
registered mail
courrier recommandé m
registration form
formulaire d'inscription m
registration number
numéro d'immatricula-
tion m
relative, relation
parent m, famille f
remain rester
remember se souvenir,
se rappeler
rent (n) location f
rent (vb) louer
repair réparer

repeat répéter
reply répondre
report (n) rapport m
report (vb) rapporter
request (n) demande f
request (vb) demander
require avoir besoin, demander
rescue (n) secours m
rescue (vb) secourir
reservation réservation f
reserve (n) réserve f
reserve (vb) réserver
resident résident(e)
resort station de vacances f
rest (relaxation) repos m
rest (remainder) reste m
rest (vb) se reposer
retired retraité(e)
return (n) retour m
return (vb) revenir
return ticket billet de retour, aller-retour m
reverse reculer
reverse charge call PCV
reverse gear marche arrière f
revolting dégoûtant(e) (dirty), révoltant(e)
rheumatism rhumatisme m
Rhine Rhin m
rib côte f

ribbon ruban m
rice riz m
rich riche
ride (n) promenade f
ride (vb) monter à cheval
ridiculous ridicule
right (correct) juste
right (direction) droite f
right-hand drive conduite à droite f
ring (n) bague f
ring (vb) sonner
ring road périphérique m
rip-off escroquerie f
ripe mür(e), fait (cheese)
river rivière f, fleuve m
road route f
road accident accident de la route m
road map carte routière f
road sign panneau indicateur m
roadworks travaux m
rock (n) roc m, rocher m
roll (n) rouleau m, petit pain (food) m
roll (vb) rouler
roof toit m
roof-rack galerie f
room pièce f, place f
rope corde f
rose rose f
rotten pourri(e)

ENGLISH → FRENCH

rough brutal(e), rugueux/rugueuse (surface)
roughly en gros, approximativement
round rond(e)
roundabout détour m
row (n) rangée f
royal royal(e)
rubber gomme f, caoutchouc m
rubbish détritus m, ordures f
rubella rubéole f
rudder gouvernail m
rug carpette f, couverture f
ruin ruine f
ruler règle f
rum rhum m
run (vb) courir
rush (vb) se précipiter
rusty rouillé(e)
rye bread pain de seigle m

S
sad triste
saddle selle f
safe (adj) sûr(e), sans danger
safe (n) coffre-fort m
safety pin épingle de sûreté f
sail voile f
sailing navigation de plaisir f
salad salade f

salad dressing vinaigrette f, mayonnaise f
sale vente f, soldes m
salesperson vendeur/ vendeuse
sales representative représentant(e) de commerce
salmon saumon m
salt sel m
same même
sand sable m
sandals sandales fpl
sandwich sandwich m
sanitary pads serviettes hygiéniques fpl
Saturday samedi m
sauce sauce f
saucer soucoupe f
sausage saucisse f
save économiser
savoury non-sucré(e), salé(e)
say dire
scales balance f
scenery paysage m
scent parfum m
school école f
scissors ciseaux m
Scot Écossais(e)
Scotland Écosse f
Scottish écossais(e)
scrambled eggs œufs brouillés m
scratch (n) égratignure f

scratch (vb) se gratter

screen écran m

screw vis f

screwdriver tournevis m

scrubbing brush brosse à récurer f

scuba diving plongée sous-marine f

sea mer f

seagull mouette f

seasickness mal de mer m

seaside bord de la mer m

season saison f

season ticket carte d'abonnement f

seasoning assaisonnement m

seat siège m, place f

seat belt ceinture de sécurité f

seaweed algue f

secluded retiré(e)

second deuxième, second(e)

second class deuxième classe f

second-hand d'occasion

secretary secrétaire m/f

security guard garde m

see voir

self-catering appartement-hôtel m

self-employed indépendant(e), à son compte

self-service libre-service m

sell vendre

sell-by date date limite de vente f, date de péremption f

send envoyer

senior citizen personne âgée, du troisième âge m

sentence phrase f, sentence f

separate (vb) séparer

September septembre

septic septique

septic tank fosse septique f

serious sérieux/ sérieuse

service (n) service m

service charge service m

set menu menu fixe m

several plusieurs

sew coudre

sex sexe m

shade ombre f

shake secouer

shallow peu profond(e)

shame honte f

shampoo and set shampooing et mise en plis m

share (vb) partager

ENGLISH → FRENCH

sharp pointu(e), tranchant(e)

shave (vb) raser

she elle

sheep mouton m

sheet drap m

shelf étagère f

shellfish crustacés m, fruits de mer m

sheltered abrité(e)

shine (vb) briller

shingle galet m

shingles zona m

ship bateau m, navire m

shirt chemise f

shock absorber amortisseur m

shoe chaussure f

shoelaces lacets (de chaussures) m

shop boutique f, magasin m

shop assistant vendeur/vendeuse

shop window vitrine f

shopping centre centre commercial m

shore rivage m

short court(e), petit(e)

short cut raccourci m

short-sighted myope

shorts short m

shoulder épaule f

shout (vb) crier

show (n) spectacle m

show (vb) montrer

shower douche f

shrimp crevette f

shrink (vb) rétrécir

shut (vb) fermer

shutter volet m

shy timide

sick malade

side côté m

side dish garniture f

sidewalk trottoir m

sieve tamis de cuisine m, passoire f

sight vue f

sightseeing excursion f

sign (n) signe m

sign (vb) signer

signal signal m

signature signature f

signpost poteau indicateur m

silence silence m

silk soie f

silly bête, idiot(e)

silver argent m

similar similaire

simple simple

sing chanter

singer chanteur/chanteuse

single seul(e), célibataire

single bed lit à une place m

single room chambre pour une personne f

sink (n) évier m

sister sœur f

sister-in-law belle-sœur f

sit s'asseoir

size taille (clothing) **f**, pointure (shoes) **f**
skate (n) patin **m**
skate (vb) faire du patinage
skating rink patinoire **f**
ski (n) ski **m**
ski (vb) skier, faire du ski
ski boots chaussures de ski **fpl**
ski jump tremplin (de ski) **m**
ski slope piste (de ski) **f**
skin peau **f**
skirt jupe **f**
sky ciel **m**
sledge traîneau **m**, luge **f**
sleep dormir
sleeper, sleeping car wagon-lit **m**
sleeping bag sac de couchage **m**
sleeping pill somnifère **m**
sleepy (to be) avoir sommeil
slice (n) tranche **f**, morceau **m**
slide (vb) glisser
slip (n) combinaison **f**, fond de robe **m**
slippers pantoufles **f**
slippery glissant(e)
Slovak slovaque, Slovaque
Slovakia Slovaquie **f**
slow lent(e)

slowly lentement
small petit(e)
smell (n) odeur **f**
smell (vb) sentir
smile (n) sourire **m**
smile (vb) sourire
smoke (n) fumée **f**
smoke (vb) fumer
smoked salmon saumon fumé **m**
snack casse-croûte **m**, amuse-gueule **m**
snake serpent **m**
sneeze (vb) éternuer
snore ronfler
snorkel (n) tuba **m**
snow, it is snowing neige **f**, il neige
soap savon **m**
soap powder lessive **f**, poudre à laver **f**
sober sobre
socket (electric) prise de courant
socks socquettes **f**
soda soda **m**
soft doux/douce
soft drink boisson non-alcoolisée
sole (fish) sole **f**
sole (shoe) semelle **f**
soluble soluble
some du, de la, des, quelques
somebody, someone quelqu'un
something quelque chose

ENGLISH → FRENCH

somewhere quelque part
son fils m
son-in-law gendre m
song chanson f
sore, it is sore douloureux/ douloureuse, ça fait mal
sore throat mal de gorge m
sorry! pardon!
sort sorte f
soup soupe f
sour aigre, acide
south sud m
South Africa Afrique du Sud f
South African sud-africain(e), Sud-Africain(e)
souvenir souvenir m
spa station thermale f
spade bêche f
Spain Espagne f
Spaniard Espagnol(e)
Spanish espagnol(e)
spanner clé à molette f
spare part pièce de rechange f
spare tyre pneu de secour m
spare wheel roue de secour f
spark plug bougie f
sparkling pétillant(e)
sparkling water eau gazeuse f
speciality spécialité f

spectacles lunettes f
speed vitesse f
speed limit limitation de vitesse f
speedometer compteur de vitesse m
spell (vb) épeler
spend dépenser
spice épice m
spider araignée f
spill (vb) renverser
spin-dryer essoreuse f
spinach épinard m
spine colonne vertébrale f
spirits alcool m
splinter écharde f
spoil gâter
spoke (n) rayon m
sponge éponge f
spoon cuillère f
sprain (n) entorse f, foulure f
spring printemps m
square (adj) carré(e)
square (n) place f
stadium stade m
stain (n) tache f
stairs escalier m
stale pas frais, rassis
stalls orchestre m
stamp timbre m
staple (vb) agrafer
star (film) star f
star (sky) étoile f, vedette
start (vb) commencer, démarrer (car)

starter (car) starter m
starter (food) hors
　d'œuvre m
station gare f
stationer's papeterie f
statue statue f
stay rester, habiter
steal voler
steam vapeur f
steep raide
steer diriger
steering wheel
　volant m
step (n) pas m
stepfather beau-
　père m
stepmother belle-
　mère f
stew ragoût m
stick (vb) coller
sticking plaster
　sparadrap m
still toujours
sting (n) piqûre f
sting (vb) piquer
stitch (n) point de
　suture (medical) m,
　point (sewing) m
stitch (vb) suturer
　(medical), coudre
　(sewing)
stock réserve f,
　bouillon m
stocking bas m
stolen volé(e)
stomach estomac m
stomachache brûlure
　d'estomac f

stone pierre f
stop (n) stop m
stop (vb) s'arrêter
stopover escale f
store (n) magasin m
store (vb)
　emmagasiner
storey étage m
storm tempête f
straight droit(e)
straight on tout droit
straightaway tout de
　suite
strange étrange
stranger étranger/
　étrangère
strap courroie f
straw paille f
strawberry fraise f
stream ruisseau m
street rue f
street map plan des
　rues m
strike (n) grève f
string ficelle f
striped à raies
stroke (n) attaque
　d'apoplexie f
strong fort(e)
stuck collé(e), coincé(e)
student étudiant(e)
student discount tarif
　étudiant m
stuffed farci(e)
stupid stupide
subtitle sous-titre m
suburb banlieue f
subway métro m

suddenly soudain
suede daim m
sugar sucre m
sugar-free sans sucre
suit costume (man) m, tailleur (woman) m
suitcase valise f
summer été m
summit sommet m
sun soleil m
sun block écran solaire m
sunburn coup de soleil m
Sunday dimanche m
sunglasses lunettes de soleil f
sunny ensoleillé(e)
sunrise lever du soleil m
sunroof toit ouvrant m
sunset coucher de soleil m
sunshade parasol m, ombrelle f
sunshine rayon de soleil m
sunstroke insolation f
suntan bronzage m
suntan lotion lotion solaire f
supper dîner m
supplement supplément m
sure sûr(e)
surfboard planche de surf f

surgery (doctor's rooms) cabinet de consultation m
surgery (procedure) opération chirurgicale f
surname nom m
surrounded entouré(e)
suspension suspension f
swallow (vb) avaler
swear jurer
swear word juron m
sweat (n) sueur f
sweat (vb) transpirer
sweater pull m
Sweden Suède f
Swedish suédois(e), Suédois(e)
sweet (adj) doux/douce, sucré(e)
sweet (n) bonbon m
swell enfler
swelling enflure f
swim nager
swimming costume maillot de bain m
swing (n) balançoire f
Swiss suisse, Suisse/Suissesse
switch (n) interrupteur m
switch off éteindre
switch on allumer
Switzerland Suisse f
synagogue synagogue f

T

table table f
table wine vin de table m
tablecloth nappe f
tablespoon cuillère à soupe f
tailor tailleur m
take prendre
takeaway food plats à emporter mpl
talcum powder talc m
talk (vb) parler
tall grand(e) (person), haut(e) (building)
tampon tampon m
tan bronzage m
tangerine mandarine f
tank réservoir m
tape cassette f
tape measure centimètre m
tape recorder magnétophone m
taste (n) goût m
taste (vb) goûter
tax taxe f, impôt m
taxi taxi m
taxi driver chauffeur de taxi m
taxi rank station de taxis
tea thé m
tea bag sachet de thé m
teach enseigner
teacher professeur m/f
team équipe f

teapot théière f
tear (n) larme (crying) f
tear (vb) déchirer
teaspoon cuillère à café f
teat tétine (bottle) f
teeth dents f
telephone téléphone m
telephone call appel téléphonique m, coup de téléphone m
television télévision f
tell dire
temperature température f
temple temple m
temporary temporaire
tendon tendon m
tennis tennis m
tennis court court de tennis m
tennis racket raquette de tennis f
tent tente f
tent peg piquet de tente m
terminal (adj) terminal(e)
terminal (n) terminus m
thank remercier
that que, qui, ça
the le, la, les
theatre théâtre m
theft vol m
there là
thermometer thermomètre f
they ils/elles

thick épais/épaisse
thief voleur/voleuse
thigh cuisse f
thin mince
thing chose f
think penser
third-party insurance
  assurance au tiers f
thirsty (to be) avoir soif
this ce, cet, cette, ceci
thorn épine f
those ces, ceux/celles,
  ceux-là/celles-là
thousand mille
thread fil m
throat gorge f
throat lozenges
  pastilles pour la
  gorge fpl
through par, à travers
throw jeter
thumb pouce m
thunder tonnerre m
thunderstorm orage m
Thursday jeudi m
ticket ticket m, billet m
ticket: single, return
  aller m, aller-retour m
ticket collector
  contrôleur/contrôleuse
ticket office guichet de
  vente des billets m
**tide, low tide, high
  tide** marée f, marée
  basse, marée haute f
tie (n) cravate f
tie (vb) attacher
tight serré(e)

tights collants m
till (cash register)
  caisse f
till (until) jusqu'à
time, what time is it?
  temps m, quelle heure
  est-il?
timetable horaire
  (railways) m, emploi du
  temps m
tin boîte f
tin opener ouvre-
  boîte m
tinfoil papier
  d'aluminium m
tiny minuscule
tip (n) pourboire m
tired fatigué(e)
tissue kleenex m,
  mouchoir en papier m
to à
today aujourd'hui
toe orteil m
together ensemble
toilet toilettes f
toll, toll road péage m,
  route à péage f
tomato tomate f
tomato juice jus de
  tomate m
tomorrow demain
tomorrow afternoon
  demain après-midi
tomorrow evening
  demain soir
tomorrow morning
  demain matin
tongue langue f

tonight ce soir
tonsillitis angine f
too aussi
tool outil m
tool kit trousse à outils f
tooth dent f
toothache mal de dents m
toothpick cure-dents m
top haut m, sommet m
top floor dernier étage m
topless seins nus
torch lampe de poche f
torn déchiré(e)
total (adj) total(e)
total (n) total m
tough solide, dur(e)
tour tour m, excursion f
tour guide guide touristique m
tour operator tour-opérateur m
tow remorquer
towel serviette de toilette f
tower tour f
town ville f
town hall mairie f, hôtel de ville m
toy jouet m
tracksuit survêtement m
traffic circulation f
traffic jam embouteillage m, bouchon m

traffic light feu m
trailer remorque f
train train m
tram tramway m, tram m
tranquiliser tranquillisant m
translate traduire
translation traduction f
translator traducteur/traductrice
trash ordures f
travel (n) voyage m
travel (vb) voyager
travel agent agent de voyages m
travel document titre de transport m
travel sickness mal des transports m
traveller's cheque chèque de voyage m, traveller's chèque m
tray plateau m
tree arbre m
trolley chariot m
trouble trouble m
trousers pantalon m
trout truite f
truck camion m
true vrai(e)
trunk malle f
try, try on essayer
tuna thon m
tunnel tunnel m
turkey dinde f
Turkey Turquie f

Turkish, Turk turc/
  turque, Turc/Turque
turn, turn around
  tourner, se retourner,
  faire demi-tour (car)
turn off éteindre, fermer
turquoise turquoise f
tweezers pince à
  épiler f
twice deux fois
twin beds lits
  jumeaux **mpl**
twins jumeaux **m**,
  jumelles **f**
type type **m**
typical typique
tyre pneu **m**
tyre pressure pression
  des pneus **f**

U
ugly laid(e)
U.K. Royaume-Uni **m**
ulcer ulcère **m**
umbrella parapluie **m**
uncle oncle **m**
uncomfortable
  inconfortable
unconscious sans
  connaissance,
  évanoui(e)
under sous
underdone saignant(e)
underground (n)
  métro **m**
underpants slip **m**,
  caleçon **m**

understand
  comprendre
underwear sous-
  vêtement **m**
unemployed au
  chômage **m**
United States États-
  Unis **mpl**
university université **f**
unleaded petrol
  essence sans plomb **f**
unlimited illimité(e)
unlock ouvrir
unpack déballer
unscrew dévisser
until jusqu'à
unusual inhabituel(le),
  étrange
up, to get up se lever
up-market haut de
  gamme
upside down à l'envers
upstairs en haut
urgent urgent(e)
us nous
use (vb) utiliser
useful utile
usual, usually
  habituel(le),
  habituellement

V
vacancy vacance **f**
vacation vacances **fpl**
vaccination vaccin **m**
vacuum cleaner
  aspirateur **m**
valid valide

valley vallée f
valuables (n) objets de valeur mpl
value (n) valeur f
valve soupape f
van camionnette f
vanilla vanille f
VAT TVA f
veal veau m
vegetable légume m
vegetarian végétarien(ne)
vehicle véhicule m
vein veine f
vending machine distributeur automatique m
venereal disease maladie vénérienne f
very très
vest tricot de corps m
vet (veterinarian) vétérinaire m/f
via via
view vue f
village village m
vinegar vinaigre m
vineyard vignoble m
violet violette f
virus virus m
visa visa m
visit (n) visite f
visit (vb) visiter
voice voix f
volcano volcan m
voltage voltage m
vomit (vb) vomir
voucher bon m

W
wage salaire m
waist taille f
waistcoat gilet m
wait attendre
waiter/waitress serveur/serveuse
waiting room salle d'attente f
wake up se réveiller
wake-up call réveil téléphonique m
Wales Pays de Galles m
walk (n) promenade f
walk (vb) marcher
wall mur m
wallet porte-feuille m
walnut noix f
want vouloir
war guerre f
ward salle (hospital) f
wardrobe penderie f, garde-robe f
warehouse entrepôt m
warm chaud(e)
wash laver, se laver
washbasin lavabo m
washing powder lessive f
washing-up liquid produit pour la vaisselle m
wasp guêpe f
waste (n) déchets m
waste bin poubelle f
watch (n) montre f
watch (vb) montrer

ENGLISH → FRENCH

watch strap bracelet de montre **m**
water eau **f**
water skiing ski nautique **m**
watermelon pastèque **f**
waterproof étanche, imperméable
wave (n) vague **f**
way, this way chemin **m**, par là
we nous
weak faible
wear porter
weather temps **m**
weather forecast prévision météorologique **f**
web web **m**, toile **f**
wedding mariage **m**
wedding present cadeau de mariage **m**
wedding ring alliance **f**
Wednesday mercredi **m**
week, last/next la semaine dernière/ prochaine **f**
week, this cette semaine **f**
weekday jour ouvrable **m**
weekend week-end **m**
weekly hebdomadaire
weigh peser
weight poids **m**
weird bizarre

welcome (adj) bienvenu(e)
welcome (n) bienvenue **f**
welcome (vb) accueillir
well (adj) bien
Welsh gallois(e), Gallois(e)
were étions, étiez, étaient
west ouest **m**
wet mouillé(e)
wetsuit combinaison de plongée **f**
what? pardon?
wheel roue **f**
wheel clamp sabot **m**
wheelchair fauteuil roulant **m**
when? quand?
where? où?
which? quel/quelle?
which one? lequel/ laquelle?
while pendant que
whipped cream crème fouettée **f**
white blanc/blanche
who? qui?
whole tout/toute, entier/entière
wholemeal bread pain complet
whose? à qui?
why? pourquoi?
wide large
widow, widower veuve/veuf

wife femme, épouse f
wig perruque f
win gagner
wind vent m
window fenêtre f
window seat place côté fenêtre f
windscreen pare-brise m
windscreen wiper essuie-glace m
windy (it is) il fait du vent
wine vin m
wine list carte des vins f
winter hiver m
wire câble m
wish (n) vœu m
wish (vb) souhaiter
with avec
without sans
witness (n) témoin m
wolf loup m
woman femme f
wood bois m
wool laine f
word mot m
work (n) travail m
work (vb) travailler
world monde m
worried inquiet/inquiète
worse pire
worth (n) valeur f
wrap up envelopper
wrapping paper papier d'emballage m, papier cadeau m

wrong faux/fausse
wrong, what is wrong? qu'est-ce qui ne va pas?

X
X-ray radiographie f, rayons X mpl

Y
yacht yacht m, voilier m
year an m, année f
yellow jaune
Yellow Pages Pages Jaunes fpl
yes oui
yesterday hier
yolk jaune d'œuf m
you vous/tu
young jeune
your votre, vos, ton, ta, tes
youth hostel auberge de jeunesse f

Z
zero zéro m
zip fastener, zipper fermeture éclair f
zone zone f
zoo zoo m

ENGLISH → FRENCH

FRENCH → ENGLISH

A

à to

à cause de because

à côté beside

à l'envers upside down

à l'étranger abroad

à l'extérieur outside

à l'intérieur indoors, inside

à la mode fashionable

à nouveau again

à peine hardly

à point medium rare (meat)

à quatre roues motrices four-wheel drive

à qui? whose?

à raies striped

à son compte self employed

à tarif réduit cheap rate

à travers through

à votre (ta) santé! cheers!

abbaye f abbey

abcès m abscess

abeille f bee

aboyer bark (vb)

abrité(e) sheltered

absent(e) off

absolument absolutely

accélérateur m accelerator

accent m accent

accepter accept

accident m accident

accident de la route m road accident

accord m agreement

accueillir welcome (vb)

acheter buy

acide sour

acompte m deposit

acte (m) de naissance birth certificate

adapté(e) fit

adapter adapt

addition f bill

adulte m/f adult

aéroglisseur m hovercraft

aéroport m airport

affaires fpl business

affiche f poster

Afrique du Sud f South Africa

âge m age

agenda m diary

agent de police m/f policeman/woman

agent de voyages m travel agent

agent immobilier estate agent

agneau m lamb

agrafer staple (vb)

agrandissement m enlargement

agréable nice

agressé(e) mugged

aider help (vb)

aigle m eagle

aigre sour

aiguille f needle
aiguille à tricoter f knitting needle
aiguille hypo-dermique f hypo-dermic needle
ail m garlic
aimant m magnet
aimer like (vb), love (vb)
air m air
aire de jeux f playground
alcool m spirits
algue f seaweed
aliment pour bébés m baby food
alimentation f food
allant au four ovenproof
allée f aisle seat, lane
allégé(e) low fat
Allemagne f Germany
allemand(e), Alle-mand(e) German
aller go (on foot)
aller m single ticket
aller chercher fetch
aller-retour m return ticket
alliance f wedding ring
allumage m ignition
allumer switch on
allumettes fpl matches
Alpes fpl Alps
alpinisme m mountaineering
amande f almond
ambassade f embassy

ambre m amber
ambulance f ambulance
améliorer improve
amener bring
ami m boyfriend
amical(e) friendly
ami(e) friend
amie f girlfriend
amorce f bait
amortisseur m shock absorber
amour m love (n)
ampoule f blister, bulb (electric)
ampoule électrique f lightbulb
amusant(e) funny
amuse-gueule m snack
amusement m fun
an m year
analgésique m painkiller
ananas m pineapple
ancien ancient
anesthésique m anaesthetic
angine f tonsillitis
anglais(e) English
Anglais(e) Englishman/woman
Angleterre f England
anguille f eel
animal m animal
animal familier m pet
année f year

anniversaire m
birthday
**anniversaire de
mariage** m wedding
anniversary
annoncer advertise
annuaire m phone
directory
annuel annual
annulation f
cancellation
annuler cancel
anthracite charcoal
(colour)
antiacide m antacid
antique ancient
aphte m mouth ulcer
appareil acoustique m
hearing aid
**appareil de
chauffage** f heater
appartement m flat (n)
appartement-hôtel m
self-catering
appat m bait
appel m call (n)
appel en PCV m
collect call
**appel longue
distance** m long-
distance call
appel téléphonique m
telephone call
appeler call (vb)
appendicite f
appendicitis
apporter bring
apprendre learn

approximativement
about, approximately,
roughly
après after, afterwards
après-midi m
afternoon
araignée f spider
arbre m tree
argent m money, silver
arranger arrange
arrêt d'autobus m
bus stop
arrêter arrest (vb)
arrhes f deposit
arrivée f arrival
arriver happen
art m art
articulation f joint
artisanat m craft
ascenseur m lift (n),
elevator
aspirateur m vacuum
cleaner
assaisonnement m
dressing (salad),
seasoning
assez enough, fairly
assiette f plate
assurance f insurance
assurance au tiers f
third-party insurance
assurance médicale f
medical insurance
assurance vie f life
insurance
asticot m maggot
astucieuse clever
astucieux clever

attacher fasten, tie (vb)
**attachez votre
  ceinture** fasten your
  seat belt
attaque f attack (n)
attaque d'apoplexie f
  stroke (n)
attendre expect, wait
attraper catch
au chômage m
  unemployed
au-delà beyond
au dessus above
au fond at the bottom
au lieu de instead
au revoir goodbye
Au secours! Help!
aube f dawn
auberge f hostel, inn
**auberge de
  jeunesse f**
  youth hostel
aucun(e) none
audience f audience
aujourd'hui today
aussi also, too
authentique genuine
autobus m bus
automne m autumn
autoroute f freeway,
  motorway
autre other
autrement otherwise
avalanche f avalanche
avaler swallow (vb)
avance advance
avant before
avarié(e) off (food)

avec with
avec un peu d'espoir
  hopefully
avenue f avenue
avenir m future (time)
avertisseur m horn
  (car)
aveugle blind (adj)
avion m plane,
  aeroplane
avoine f oats
avoir get, have
avoir besoin need (vb),
  require
avoir de la chance
  lucky (to be)
avoir faim hungry
avoir peur de to be
  afraid of
avoir soif to be thirsty
avoir sommeil to be
  sleepy
avortement m abortion

B
bacon m bacon
bagage m baggage,
  luggage
bague f ring (n)
baie f bay
baignoire f bath
bail m lease
bain m bath
bain de bouche m
  mouthwash
baiser m kiss (n)
balai m broom
balance f scales

FRENCH → ENGLISH

143

balançoire f swing (n)
balcon m balcony
bandage m bandage
banlieue f suburb
bar pour homo-sexuels m gay bar
barbe f beard
barrière f fence, gate
bas m stocking
bas/basse low
bas-côté m aisle
bassin m pool
bataille f fight (n)
bateau m boat, ship
bâtiment m building
batterie à plat flat battery
beau beautiful, handsome
beau-frère m brother-in-law
beau-père m father-in-law, stepfather
beaucoup lot (adv), much
beaucoup (de) many
beaux-parents mpl parents-in-law
bêche f spade
bed & breakfast m bed & breakfast
beignet m doughnut
belle beautiful
belle-fille f daughter-in-law
belle-mère f mother-in-law, stepmother

belle-sœur f sister-in-law
béquilles f crutches
berceau m cot
besoin m need (n)
bête silly
beurre m butter
bibliothèque f library
bidon d'essence petrol can
bien well (adj)
bien portant(e) healthy
bien que although
bienvenu(e) welcome (adj)
bienvenue f welcome (n)
bière à la pression f draught beer
bière blonde f lager
bijouterie f jewellery
bijoutier m jeweller
billet m ticket
billet d'avion m air ticket
billet de retour m return ticket
billet open m open ticket
billetterie f auto-teller
bio(logique) organic (vegetables)
biscuit m biscuit, cookie
bise f kiss (n)
bizarre odd, peculiar, weird
blanc/blanche white
blessé(e) injured

blessure f injury
bleu m bruise
bleu(e) blue
bloc-note m notebook, notepaper
blond(e) fair (hair colour)
bloqué(e) blocked
blouse f blouse
bobine f coil (n)
bocal m jar
bœuf m beef
boire drink (vb)
bois m wood
boisson f drink (n)
boisson non-alcoolisée soft drink
boîte f box, can (n), tin
boîte à fusibles f fuse box
boîte à lettres f letterbox
boîte de vitesses f gearbox
boîte en carton f carton
boîte postale f post box
bol m bowl
bon m voucher
bon/bonne good
bon marché cheap
bonbon m candy, sweet (n)
bonde f plug (sink)
bonjour good morning, good afternoon, good day

Bonne Année! Happy New Year!
bonne chance good luck
bonne d'enfants f nanny
bonne nuit good night
bonsoir good evening
bord m edge
bord de la mer m seaside
bottes fpl boots
bouche f mouth
bouchée f bite (n, food)
boucher m butcher
bouchon m cork, traffic jam
bouclé(e) curly
boucles d'oreilles f earrings
boue f mud
bouée de sauvetage f lifebelt
bouger move (vb)
bougie f candle, spark plug
bouillir boil (vb)
bouilloire f kettle
bouillon m stock
bouillotte f hot-water bottle
boulangerie f bakery
boulot m job
bouquet m bunch
boussole f compass
bout m bit
bouteille f bottle, flask

FRENCH → ENGLISH

bouteille de gaz f gas cylinder
boutique f shop
bouton m button
boutons de manchettes m cufflinks
bracelet m bracelet
bracelet de montre m watch strap
branche branch
brandy m brandy
brasserie f brewery, restaurant
bretelle de contournement f bypass (road)
brillant bright
briller shine
brioche f bun
briquet m cigarette lighter
brise f breeze
britannique/ Britannique British
broche f brooch
brochure f brochure
bronchite f bronchitis
bronzage m suntan, tan
brosse f brush
brosse à cheveux f hairbrush
brosse à ongles f nail brush
brosse à récurer f scrubbing brush
brouillard m fog

bruit m noise
brûler burn
brûlure d'estomac f heartburn, stomach ache
brume f mist
brun(e) brown (hair)
brutal(e) rough
Bruxelles Brussels
bruyant(e) loud, noisy
buggy m buggy
buisson m bush
bulbe m bulb (plant)
bureau m desk, office
bureau de change m bureau de change
bureau de poste m post office
bureau des renseignements m enquiry desk
bus m bus

C

ça that
ça fait mal it is sore
ça va? how are you? (informal)
cabillaud m cod
cabine f cabin
cabine téléphonique f phone booth
cabinet de consultation m surgery (doctor's rooms)
câble m wire

câbles de démarrage m
jump leads

cacahuète f peanut

cacao m cocoa

cacher hide (vb)

cadeau m present (n), gift

cadeau d'anniversaire m
birthday present

cadeau de mariage m
wedding present

cadenas m padlock

cadre m frame

cadre à photo m
picture frame

cafard m cockroach

café m coffee

café glacé m iced coffee

café instantané m
instant coffee

caisse f case, cash desk, till

caissier m cashier

caissière f cashier

cake m fruitcake

calculette f calculator

caleçon m underpants

calmant m painkiller

calme calm

cambriolage m
break-in, burglary

cambrioleur m burglar

camion m lorry, truck

camionnette f van

campagne f countryside

camper camp (vb)

camping pour caravanes m
caravan site

Canada m Canada

canal m canal

canalisation f drain (n)

canapé m couch

canard m duck

cancer m cancer

canne à pêche f
fishing rod

canoë m canoe

canot automobile m
motorboat

caoutchouc m rubber

capital m capital (finance)

capitale f capital (city)

capot m bonnet (car)

capuchon m hood

car m bus, coach

caravane f caravan

carburant m fuel

carburateur m carburettor

cardigan m cardigan

carnet m notebook, notepaper

carotte f carrot

carpette f rug

carré(e) square (adj)

carrefour m crossroads

carte f card, map

FRENCH → ENGLISH

carte d'abonnement f
season ticket
carte d'anniversaire f
birthday card
**carte d'embarque-
ment f** boarding card
carte d'identité f
identity card
**carte d'identité
bancaire f** cheque
card
carte de crédit f
charge card, credit card
carte des vins f wine
list
carte postale f
postcard
carte routière f road
map
carton m cardboard
casier m locker
casque m helmet
**casque de
protection m**
crash helmet
casquette f cap
cassable breakable
casse-croûte m snack
casser break (vb)
casserole f pan
cassette f cassette
tape
cassis m blackcurrants
catastrophe f disaster
cathédrale f cathedral
catholique Catholic
cave f cellar
CE f EC

ce it, this
ce matin this morning
ce soir tonight
ceci this
ceinture f belt
ceinture de sécurité f
seat belt
ceinture-portefeuille f
money belt
célèbre famous
céleri m celery
célibataire single
centigrade m
Centigrade
centimètre m tape
measure, centimetre
centre m centre
centre commercial m
shopping centre
centre-ville m city
centre
cercle m circle
cerise f cherry
certain(e) certain
certainement certainly,
definitely
certificat m certificate
c'est it is
c'est combien? how
much is it?
c'est dommage
it's a pity
**c'est sans
importance**
it doesn't matter
c'est tout nothing else
ces those
cet this

cette this
cette semaine f this week
ceux/celles those
ceux-là/celles-là those
chacun(e) everyone
chaîne f channel (TV), chain
chaise f chair
chaise haute pour enfants f high chair
chaise longue f deck chair
chaleur f heat
chambre à air f inner tube
chambre et petit déjeuner f bed & breakfast
chambre pour deux personnes f double room
chambre pour une personne f single room
champ m field
champ de course m racecourse
Champagne m Champagne
champignon m mushroom
chance f luck
changer change (vb)
chanson f song
chanter sing

chanteur/chanteuse singer
chapeau m hat
chapelle f chapel
chaque each
charbon m coal
charbon de bois m charcoal
chariot m trolley
chariot à bagages m luggage trolley
charpentier m carpenter
charter m charter flight
chasse f hunt (n)
chat m cat
châtaigne f chestnut
château m castle
chaud(e) hot, warm
chauffage m heating
chauffe-eau m water heater
chauffeur m driver
chauffeur de taxi m taxi driver
chaussure f shoe
chaussures de ski fpl ski boots
check-in m check-in
chef chef
chemin m path, way
chemin de fer m railway
cheminée f chimney
chemise f shirt
chemise de nuit f nightdress

FRENCH → ENGLISH

FRENCH → ENGLISH

chêne m oak
chèque m cheque
chèque de voyage m
traveller's cheque
chéquier m cheque
book
cher/chère dear,
expensive
chercher look for
cherry m cherry brandy
cheval m horse
cheveux m hair
cheville f ankle
chèvre f goat
chewing-gum m
chewing gum
chic m/f posh
chiffon m cloth, rag
Chine f China
chinois(e), Chinois(e)
Chinese
chips m chips, crisps
chocolat m
chocolate
chocolats m
chocolates
chœur m choir
choisir choose
chope f mug
chose f thing
chou m cabbage
chou-fleur m
cauliflower
chute f fall (n)
ciboulette f chives
cidre m cider
ciel m sky
cigare m cigar

cigarette f cigarette
cimetière m cemetery
cinéma m cinema
cintre hanger, coat
hanger
circulation f traffic
ciseaux mpl scissors
ciseaux à ongles mpl
nail scissors
citerne f cistern
citoyen(ne) citizen
citron m lemon
citron vert m lime
clair bright, clear
claire clear, bright
classe f class
classe économie f
economy class
clavicule f collarbone
clé f key
clé à molette f
spanner
clé de contact f
ignition key
client(e) customer
clignotant m indicator
climatisation f air
conditioning
clinique f clinic
cloche f bell
club de golfe m golf
club
Coca-Cola m Coke
cochon m pig
code m code
code postal m postal
code
cœur m heart

coffre m boot (car)
coffre-fort m safe (n)
cogner hit (vb)
coiffeur m hairdresser
coiffeuse f hairdresser
coin m corner
coincé(e) jammed, stuck
col m collar
colis m packet, parcel
collant m pantyhose, tights
colle f glue
collé(e) stuck
collecter collect (vb)
collègue m/f colleague
coller stick (vb)
collier m necklace
collision f crash
colonne vertébrale f spine
combien? how much? how many?
combinaison f slip (n)
combinaison de plongée f wetsuit
combiné receiver (phone)
comédie f comedy
commande f order (n)
commander order (vb)
comme like
commencer start (vb)
comment? how?
comment allez-vous? how are you? (formal)

commissariat de police m police station
commode f chest of drawers
commode convenient
commotion f concussion
compagne f partner (friend)
compagnie f company
compagnon m partner (friend)
compartiment m compartment
complètement completely
composer dial (vb)
compositeur m composer
comprendre realize, understand
compris(e) included
compte m account, bill
compteur de vitesse m speedometer
comptoir m counter
concert m concert
concession f concession
concombre m cucumber
condition f condition
conduire drive (vb)
conduite à droite f right-hand drive
conférence f conference

FRENCH → ENGLISH

151

FRENCH → ENGLISH

confirmation f
confirmation
confirmer confirm
confiture f jam
confortable
comfortable
confusion f mix-up
congé m holiday, leave
congélateur m freezer
connaître know
(somebody)
conscient(e) conscious
conseiller advise
constipé(e)
constipated
construire build
consulat m consulate
contact m contact (n)
**contagieux/
contagieuse**
infectuous
contenir hold (vb)
content(e) glad
continuer continue
contraceptif m
contraceptive
contrat m contract
contravention f
parking ticket
contre against
**contrôle des laissez-
passer** m pass
control
contrôler check (vb)
**contrôleur/
contrôleuse**
ticket collector
coordonnées f details

copain m boyfriend
copie f copy (n)
coquelicot m poppy
corde f rope
corde à linge f clothes
line
corne f horn (animal)
corps m body
correctement properly
correspondance f
connection, connecting
flight
correspondant(e)
penfriend
costume m suit (man)
côte f coast, rib
côté m side
côtelette f chop (n)
coton m cotton
coton hydrophile m
cotton wool
cou m neck
couche f diaper, nappy
coucher de soleil m
sunset
couchette f couchette
coude m elbow
coudre sew, stitch (vb)
couette f duvet
couffin m carry-cot
coulant(e) fluent
couleur f colour
couloir m aisle seat,
corridor
coup de soleil m
sunburn
coup de téléphone m
telephone call

coupe f cup
coupe de cheveux f haircut
coupé(e) disconnected
couper cut (vb)
couple m couple
couramment fluently
courant m current (n)
courant d'air m draught
courber bend (vb)
courir run (vb)
couronne f crown
courrier m mail
courrier par avion m airmail
courrier recommandé m registered mail
courroie f strap
courroie de ventilateur f fan belt
cours m course
cours de langue m language course
course f race
course de chevaux f horse racing
court(e) short
court de tennis m tennis court
cousin(e) m/f cousin
coussin m cushion
coût m cost
couteau m knife
coutume f custom
couvercle m lid

couvert m cover charge
couverts m cutlery
couverture f blanket, rug
crabe m crab
crampe f cramp
cravate f tie (n)
crayon m pencil
crèche f crèche
crème f cream
crème anglaise f custard
crème fouettée f whipped cream
crème hydratante f moisturiser
crêpe f pancake
crevaison f puncture
crevette f prawn, shrimp
cri m cry (n)
cric m jack
crier cry (vb), shout (vb)
crime m crime
crise cardiaque f heart attack
cristal m crystal
croire believe
croisement m crossing
croisière f cruise
croix f cross (n)
cru(e) raw
crustacés m shellfish
cueillette harvest
cuillère f spoon
cuillère à café f teaspoon

FRENCH → ENGLISH

cuillère à soupe f
tablespoon
cuir m leather
cuisine f kitchen
cuisinier m chef (male)
cuisinière f cooker,
chef (female)
cuisinière à gaz f gas
cooker
cuisse f thigh
culotte f knickers
cure-dents m
toothpick
cuvée du patron f
house wine
cycle m cycle
cystite f cystitis

D
d'abord first
d'accord all right, OK
d'avance in advance
daim m suede
daltonien(ne) colour
blind
dame f lady
dames ladies' toilet
Danemark m Denmark
danger m danger
**dangereux/
dangereuse**
dangerous
dans in, into
danse f dance
date f date
date de naissance f
date of birth

date de péremption f
sell-by date
date limite de vente f
sell-by date
dates f dates
davantage further
dé m dice
de from, of
de la some
de la part de from
de l'après-midi p.m.
de taille moyenne
medium sized
de temps en temps
occasionally
déballer unpack
débutant(e) beginner
décaféiné
decaffeinated
décapsuleur m bottle
opener
décembre December
déchets m refuse (n),
waste (n)
déchiré(e) torn
déchirer tear (vb)
décider decide
décision f decision
décrire describe
déçu(e) disappointed
déduire deduct
défaut m fault, flaw
défectueuse faulty
défectueux faulty
défendu(e) prohibited
dégâts m damage
dégoûtant(e) filthy,
dirty, revolting

degré m degree
dehors out, outside
déjà already
déjeuner m lunch
délai m delay (n)
délibérément deliberately
délicieux/délicieuse delicious
deltaplane m hang-gliding
demain tomorrow
demain après-midi tomorrow afternoon
demain matin tomorrow morning
demain soir tomorrow evening
demande f request (n)
demande de renseignements enquiry
demander require, request, ask (vb)
démangeaison f itch
démaquillant pour les yeux m eye make-up remover
démarrer start (car)
déménager move (vb)
demi-sec medium dry (wine)
demie f half
démodé(e) old-fashioned
démolir knock down
dent f tooth
dentelle f lace

dentier m dentures
dentiste m dentist
dents f teeth
départ m departure
dépasser overtake
dépenser spend
dépenses f expenses
dépression nerveuse f nervous breakdown
dernier/dernière last
dernier étage m top floor
derrière behind
des some
désagréable nasty
descendre get off
description f description
désorienté(e) confused
dessert m dessert, pudding
dessin m drawing
dessus over
destination f destination
détachant m cleaning solution
détails m details
détergent m detergent
détour m detour, roundabout
détritus m rubbish
dettes fpl debts
deux fois twice
deuxième second

FRENCH → ENGLISH

deuxième classe f
second class
devant front, in front of
**développement de
photos** film
processing
développer develop,
print (photo)
devenir get, become
devise f currency
dévisser unscrew
devoir must, owe
diabétique diabetic
diamant diamond
diarrhée f diarrhoea
dictionnaire m
dictionary
diesel m diesel
Dieu m God
différence f difference
différent(e) different
difficile difficult
dimanche m Sunday
dinde f turkey
dîner m dinner, supper
dire say, tell
direct(e) direct (adj)
directeur m manager
direction f direction
diriger steer, direct
disparaître disappear
disponible available
dispute f quarrel
disque m record
(n, music)
**disque de stationne-
ment** m parking disk
disque dur m hard disk

dissolvant m nail polish
remover
**distributeur
automatique** m
vending machine
**distributeur
(automatique) de
billets** m auto-teller,
cash dispenser
d'occasion second-
hand
doigt m finger
domestique f maid
dommage! too bad!
dommage m damage
donner give
**donner un coup de
pied** kick (vb)
dormir sleep
dos m back
dossier m file (n),
record (n, legal)
douane f customs
double double
douche f shower
douleur f ache, pain
**douloureux/
douloureuse** sore,
painful
doux/douce soft,
sweet (adj)
douzaine f dozen
drap m sheet
drapeau m flag
dresser put ... up
drogue f drug (n)
droit(e) straight

droit d'entrée m
  admission fee,
  entrance fee
droite f right (direction)
du some
du matin a.m. (before
  noon)
du soir p.m.
du troisième âge m
  senior citizen
dur(e) hard, tough
dynamo f dynamo

E
eau f water
eau de Javel f bleach
eau gazeuse f
  sparkling water
eau potable f drinking
  water
échange m exchange
écharde f splinter
échecs m chess
échelle ladder
éclair m lightning
éclater burst
école f school
école maternelle f
  nursery school
économie f economy
économiser save
écossais(e) Scottish
Écossais(e) Scot
Écosse f Scotland
écouter listen
écouteurs m head-
  phones, earphones
écran m screen

écran solaire m sun
  block
écrémé(e) low fat
écrou m nut (for bolt)
église f church
égratignure f
  scratch (n)
élastique m elastic
  band
électricien m
  electrician
électricité f electricity
électrique electric
elle it, she
elles they (females)
emballer pack (vb)
embouteillage m
  traffic jam
embrasser kiss (vb)
embrayage m
  clutch (n)
emmagasiner
  store (vb)
émoussé blunt
emploi du temps m
  timetable
emprunter borrow
en in, into, some
en bas below, at the
  bottom, downstairs
en colère angry
en face opposite
en forme fit (health)
en grande quantité
  plenty
en gros roughly
en haut upstairs
en panne out of order

FRENCH → ENGLISH

en pente downhill
en plein air outdoors
en retard late
enceinte pregnant
enchanté(e) pleased to meet you, how do you do? (formal)
encombré(e) crowded
encore again
encre f ink
endroit m area
enfant m/f child
enfermer lock in
enfler swell
enflure f swelling
ennuyer annoy
ennuyeux boring
enquête f enquiry
enregistrement m check-in
enseigner teach
ensemble together
ensoleillé(e) sunny
ensuite afterwards, next
entendre hear
entier/entière whole
entièrement altogether
entorse f sprain (n)
entouré(e) surrounded
entraînement m practice
entrée f entrance
entrepôt m warehouse
entrer come in, enter
enveloppe f envelope
envelopper wrap up
envoyer send

épais/épaisse thick
épaule f shoulder
épeler spell (vb)
épice m spice
épicier m greengrocer
épileptique epileptic
épinard m spinach
épine f thorn
épingle f pin
épingle à linge f clothes peg
épingle de sûreté f safety pin
éplucher peel (vb)
éponge f sponge
épouse f wife
épuisé(e) exhausted
équipe f team
équipement m gear, equipment
équitablement fairly
équitation f horse riding
erreur f error, mistake
éruption f rash
escalator m escalator
escale f stopover
escalier m stairs
escalier roulant escalator
escroquerie f rip-off
Espagne f Spain
Espagnol(e) Spaniard
espagnol(e) Spanish
espèces f cash
espérance f hope
espoir m hope
esprit m mind
essayer try, try on

essence f petrol
essence sans plomb f
  unleaded petrol
essentiel(le) essential
essoreuse f spin-dryer
essuie-glace m
  windscreen wiper
est east, he/she is
estomac m stomach
Estonie f Estonia
et and
étage m floor, storey
étagère f shelf
étaient they were
étanche waterproof
États-Unis mpl
  United States
été m summer
éteindre switch off,
  turn off
éteint(e) off (switch)
éternuer sneeze (vb)
étiez you were
étions we were
étiquette f label
étiquette à bagages f
  luggage tag
étoile f star (sky)
étrange peculiar,
  strange, unusual
étranger m foreign,
  foreigner, stranger
étrangère f foreign,
  foreigner, stranger
être d'accord agree
étroit(e) narrow
étudiant(e) student
EU f EU

Europe f Europe
européen(ne)
  European
évanoui(e)
  unconscious
éventail m fan (n)
évier m sink (n)
éviter avoid
exact(e) accurate
exactement exactly
exagéré(e) overdone
examen m examination
**excédent de
  bagages** m excess
  luggage
excellent(e) excellent
excepté except
excitant(e) exciting
exclure exclude
excursion f excursion,
  sightseeing, tour
excursion en bateau f
  boat trip
excuse f apology
excusez-moi
  excuse me
exemple m example
expérimenté(e)
  experienced
expirer expire
expliquer explain
explosion f explosion
exportation f
  export (n)
exporter export (vb)
exposition f exhibition
exprès express (post)
exprimer express (vb)

FRENCH → ENGLISH

extincteur m fire extinguisher

extraordinaire extraordinary

F

fabrication f make (n)

facile easy

facteur m postman

facture f invoice

faible weak

faire make (vb)

faire cuire cook (vb)

faire demi-tour turn around (car)

faire du jogging jog

faire du patinage skate (vb)

faire du ski ski (vb)

faire du stop hitchhike

faire la queue queue (vb)

faire un brushing blow-dry

fait made, ripe (cheese)

fait à la main handmade

faites le plein fill up (petrol)

falaise f cliff

famille f family, relative, relation

farci(e) stuffed

fard à joues m blusher

farine f flour

fatigué(e) tired

faute f fault, mistake

fauteuil m armchair

fauteuil roulant m wheelchair

faux m fake (n)

faux/fausse false, wrong

favori/favorite favourite

fax m fax

félicitations f congratulations

femelle f female (animal)

féminin female (gender)

femme f wife, woman

femme de chambre f chambermaid

fenêtre f window

fer m iron (n)

fer à repasser m iron (n)

ferme f farm

fermer close, shut, turn off (vb)

fermer à clé lock (vb)

fermeture éclair f zip fastener, zipper

fermier m farmer

fermière f farmer

ferry-boat m ferry, car ferry

festival m festival

fête f party (celebration)

feu m fire, traffic light

feu de stop m brake light

février February

fiancé m fiancé

fiancé(e) engaged (to be married)

fiancée f fiancée
ficelle f string
fièvre f fever
fil m thread
fil dentaire m dental floss
filet m fillet, net
filiale f branch
fille f daughter, girl
film m film
film alimentaire m cling film
film en couleur m colour film
fils m son
filtre m filter
fin f end
finalement eventually
fines herbes f herbs
finir finish (vb)
fixer fix (vb)
flanelle f flannel
flash m flash
fleur f flower
fleuriste m/f florist
fleuve m river
foie m liver
fond de robe m slip (n)
fondre melt
fondrière f pothole
fontaine f fountain
football m football
forêt f forest
formel(le) formal
formulaire m form
formulaire d'inscription m registration form

fort(e) loud, strong
forteresse f fortress
fosse septique f septic tank
fou/folle mad
foule f crowd
foulure f sprain (n)
four m oven
four à micro-ondes m microwave (oven)
fourchette f fork
fourmi f ant
fourrure f fur
foyer m home, hostel, lobby
fracture f fracture
frais/fraîche fresh, cool
fraise f strawberry
framboise f raspberry
français(e) French
Français(e) Frenchman/woman
France f France
frapper knock (vb)
free-lance m freelance
frein m brake
frein à main m handbrake
fréquent(e) frequent
frère m brother
frigo m fridge
frire fry
frit(e) fried
frites f chips
froid(e) cold
fromage m cheese
frontière f border
fruit m fruit

fruits de mer m
shellfish
fuite f leak (n)
fumée f smoke (n)
fumer smoke (vb)
funiculaire m funicular
fusible m fuse
fusil m gun
futur m future, future
tense

G

gagner win
galerie f gallery,
roof-rack
galet m shingle
gallois(e), Gallois(e)
Welsh
gallon m gallon
gants m gloves
garage m garage
garantie f guarantee
garçon m boy
garde f guard
garde m security guard
garde-côte m
coastguard
garde-robe f wardrobe
garder keep (vb)
Gardez la monnaie!
Keep the change!
gardien(ne) caretaker
gare f station, railway
station
garniture f side dish,
filling (sandwich)
gâteau m cake
gâter spoil

gauche left
gaucher/gauchère
left-handed
gaz m gas
gazinière f gas cooker
gelé(e) frozen
gelée f frost
gênant(e) inconvenient
gendarmerie f police
station
gendre m son-in-law
général(e) general
généreux/généreuse
generous
Genève Geneva
genou m knee
gens m folk, people
gentil/gentille kind,
nice
gibier m game (animal)
gilet m waistcoat
gilet de sauvetage m
lifejacket
glace f ice, ice cream
glacier m glacier
glacière f cool bag/box
glissant(e) slippery
**glissement de
terrain** m landslide
glisser slide, slip (vb)
gomme f rubber
gorge f throat
gothique Gothic
goût m flavour, taste (n)
goûter taste (vb)
goutte f drop (n)
**gouttes pour les
yeux** f eye drops

gouvernail m rudder

gouvernement m government

graduellement gradually

grammaire f grammar

gramme m gram

grand(e) large, tall (person)

grand magasin m department store

Grande-Bretagne f Great Britain

grandiose grand

grand-mère f grandmother

grand-père m grandfather

grands-parents m grandparents

grange f barn

gras(se) fatty, greasy

gratuit(e) free

grec/grecque, Grec/ Grecque Greek

Grèce f Greece

grêle f hail

grenier m attic

grenouille f frog

grève f strike (n)

grillé(e) grilled

grimper climb (vb)

grippe f flu

gris(e) grey

gros/grosse big, fat

groseilles rouges f redcurrants

grosseur f lump

grotte f cave

groupe m group

guêpe f wasp

guerre f war

gueule de bois f hangover

guichet de vente des billets m ticket office

guide m guide

guide de conversation m phrase book

guide touristique m guide book, tour guide

guitare f guitar

gymnastique f gym

H

habillement mpl clothes

habiter stay

habituel(le) usual

habituellement usually

hall m hall

hamburger m hamburger

hanche f hip

handicapé(e) disabled, handicapped

haricot m bean

haut m top

haut(e) tall, high (building)

haut de gamme up-market

hauteur f height

hebdomadaire weekly

hélicoptère m helicopter

FRENCH → ENGLISH

herbe f grass
hernie f hernia
heure f hour
heures d'ouverture fpl
  opening times
heureusement
  fortunately
heureux/heureuse
  happy
hibou m owl
hier yesterday
hier soir last night
histoire f history
historique historic
hiver m winter
hollandais(e),
  Hollandais(e) Dutch
homard m lobster
homme m man
homme de loi m
  lawyer
hommes mpl men
hommes gents' toilet
homosexuel/le gay
Hongrie f Hungary
hongrois(e),
  Hongrois(e)
  Hungarian
honnête honest
honte f shame
hôpital m hospital
horaire m timetable
  (railways)
hors d'œuvre m
  starter (food)
hors taxes duty-free
hospitalité f hospitality

hôtel de ville m town
  hall
housse de couette f
  duvet cover
huile f oil
huile d'olive f olive oil
humide damp, humid
humour m humour
hydrofoil m hydrofoil
hypertension f high
  blood pressure

I

ici here
idée f idea
idiot(e) silly
il he, it
il fait du vent it is windy
il neige it is snowing
il pleut it is raining
il y a ago
il y a une semaine
  a week ago
île f island
illimité(e) unlimited
ils they (males)
ils/elles sont they are
image f picture
immédiatement
  immediately
immeuble m block of
  flats
impair odd (number)
imperméable m
  raincoat
imperméable
  waterproof (adj)
important(e) important

164

impossible impossible

impôt m tax

imprimer print (vb)

imprimés m printed matter

inclus(e) included

inconfortable uncomfortable

incroyable incredible

indépendant(e) self-employed, freelance

indicateur m indicator

indicatif m dialling code

indien/indienne, Indien/Indienne Indian

indigestion f indigestion

infection f infection

infirmier m male nurse

infirmière f nurse

inflammation f inflammation

information f information

ingénieur m engineer

ingrédient m ingredient

inhabituel(le) unusual

injection f injection

inondation f flood

inquiet/inquiète worried

insecte m insect

insister insist

insolation f sunstroke

insomnie f insomnia

institut de beauté m beauty salon

insuline f insulin

intelligent(e) clever, intelligent

interdit(e) forbidden, prohibited

intéressant(e) interesting

international(e) international

interprète m/f interpreter

interrupteur m switch (n)

interrupteur général m mains switch

intersection f intersection

intervalle m interval

intoxication alimentaire f food poisoning

introduire introduce

invitation f invitation

invité(e) guest

inviter invite (vb)

irlandais(e) Irish

Irlandais(e) Irishman/woman

Irlande f Ireland

Irlande du Nord f Northern Ireland

Italie f Italy

italien/italienne, Italien/Italienne Italian

ivre drunk

FRENCH → ENGLISH

FRENCH → ENGLISH

J

jaloux/jalouse jealous
jamais never
jambe f leg
jambon m ham
janvier January
jardin m garden
jauge de carburant f fuel gauge
jaune yellow
jaune d'œuf m yolk
jaunisse f jaundice
je I
je suis I am
jersey m jersey
jeter throw
jeu m game (play)
jeudi m Thursday
jeune young
joaillier m jeweller
joie f joy
joindre contact (vb), join
joli(e) lovely, pretty
jonction f junction
joue f cheek
jouer play (vb)
jouet m toy
jour m day
jour férié m public holiday
jour ouvrable m weekday
journal m newspaper
journal télévisé m news
Joyeuses Pâques! Happy Easter!

juge m judge (n)
juif/juive Jewish
Juif/Juive Jew/Jewess
juillet July
juin June
jumeaux m twins
jumelles fpl binoculars, twins
jupe f skirt
jurer swear
juriste m/f lawyer
juron m swear word
jus m juice
jus d'orange m orange juice
jus de fruit m fruit juice
jus de tomate m tomato juice
jus de viande m gravy
jusqu'à till, until
juste correct, fair, just, right

K

kilo kilo
kilogramme m kilogram
kilomètre m kilometre
kiosque m kiosk
kiosque à journaux m newsstand
kitchenette f kitchenette
kleenex m tissue
kyste m cyst

L

la her, the, it
là there
La Manche f English Channel
la semaine dernière f last week
la semaine prochaine f next week
lac m lake
lacet m lace (shoe)
lacets (de chaussures) m shoelaces
lâche loose
laid(e) ugly
lainage m knitwear
laine f wool
laisser partir let off
laisser tomber drop (vb)
laissez-passer m pass (n)
lait m milk
lait en poudre m powdered milk
laitue f lettuce
lames de rasoir fpl razor blades
lampe f lamp
lampe de poche f torch
landau m pram
langue f language, tongue
lapin m rabbit
large wide
larme f tear (n, crying)

laurier m bay leaf
lavabo m washbasin
lavage de voiture m carwash
laver wash
laverie automatique f launderette, laundromat
lavette f cloth, rag
laxatif m laxative
le him, the, it
le matin a.m. (before noon)
le plus most
leçon f lesson
lecteur de CD m CD player
léger/légère light (adj)
légume m vegetable
lent(e) slow
lentement slowly
lentille f lens
lentilles f lentils
lequel/laquelle? which one?
les the, them
lesbienne f lesbian
lessive f soap powder, washing powder
lettre f letter
lever lift (vb)
lever du soleil m sunrise
levier m lever
levier de changement de vitesse m gear lever
librairie f bookshop
libre free

libre-service m self-service

licence f licence

lièvre m hare

ligne f line

lime à ongles f nail file

limitation de vitesse f speed limit

limonade f lemonade

linge m linen

linge à laver laundry

lingerie f lingerie

lion m lion

liqueur f liqueur

liquide m cash

liquide de freins m brake fluid

lire read

liste f list

lit m bed

lit à deux places m double bed

lit à une place m single bed

litre m litre

lits jumeaux mpl twin beds

living-room m living room

livraison des bagages f baggage claim

livre f pound

livre m book (n)

livrer deliver

local m local

location f rent (n)

logement m accommodation

loi f law

loin away, far

long/longue long (adj)

lot m lot (n)

lotion solaire f suntan lotion

louer hire (vb), rent (vb), let

loup m wolf

loupe f magnifying glass

lourd(e) heavy

luge f sledge

lui to him, to her

lumière f light (n)

lundi Monday

lune f moon

lune de miel f honeymoon

lunettes f glasses, spectacles

lunettes de soleil f sunglasses

lunettes protectrices f goggles

luxe m luxury

M

ma my

machine f machine

mâchoire f jaw

Madame (Mme) Mrs

Mademoiselle (Mlle) Miss

magasin m shop, store (n)

magasin d'alimenta-tion m food shop
magasin de produits diététiques m health food shop
magazine m magazine
magnétophone m tape recorder
magnifique grand
mai May
maillot de bain m swimming costume
main f hand
maintenant now
mairie f town hall
mais but
maison f home, house
maison de ferme farmhouse
maître-nageur m lifeguard
mal badly
mal d'oreilles m earache
mal de dents m toothache
mal de dos m backache
mal de gorge m sore throat
mal de mer m seasickness
mal de tête m headache
mal des transports m travel sickness
mal du pays m homesickness

malade ill, sick
maladie f illness
maladie vénérienne f venereal disease
mâle m male (n)
malentendu m misunderstanding
malle f trunk
manager m manager
manche m handle
mandarine f tangerine
mandat-poste m money order
manger eat
mannequin m dummy, model
manquer miss (vb)
mansarde f attic
manteau m coat, overcoat
manteau de fourrure m fur coat
manuel m manual (n)
marais m marsh
marbre m marble
marché m market, deal
marche arrière f reverse gear
marché aux puces m flea market
marcher walk (vb)
marée f tide
marée basse f low tide
marée haute f high tide
mari m husband
mariage m wedding
marié m bridegroom

FRENCH → ENGLISH

FRENCH → ENGLISH

marié(e) married
mariée f bride
marine f navy
marmelade f marmalade
marque f brand
marron brown
mars March
marteau m hammer
mascara m mascara
masculin male (adj)
masque de plongée m goggles
mât m mast
match m match
match de football m football match
matelas m mattress
matériel m material
matière f matter
matin m morning
mauvais bad
mayonnaise f mayonnaise, salad dressing
me me
mécanique f mechanic
méchant(e) nasty
médicament m medicine
médiéval(e) medieval
Méditerranée f Mediterranean
méduse f jellyfish
meilleur(e) better
mélanger mix (vb)
melon m melon
même even, same

ménage m housework
mener lead (vb)
méningite f meningitis
mensuel/mensuelle monthly
mentionner mention (vb)
mentir lie
menton m chin
menu m menu
menu fixe m set menu
mer f sea
Mer du Nord f North Sea
mercredi m Wednesday
mère f mother
meringue f meringue
merveilleux/ merveilleuse great
mes my
message m message
messagerie f courier service
messe f mass
mesurer measure (vb)
métal m metal
mètre m meter
métro m metro, subway, underground (n)
meuble m furniture
meublé(e) furnished
midi midday, noon
miel m honey
mieux better
migraine f migraine
mile m mile

milieu m middle, medium
mille thousand
mince thin
minuit midnight
minuscule tiny
minute f minute (n)
miroir m mirror
mite f moth
modèle m pattern
moi me
moi-même myself
moins less
mois m month
moisson f harvest
moitié f half
mollet m calf (anatomy)
moment m moment
mon my
monastère m monastery
monde m world
monnaie f change (money)
Monsieur (M.) Mr
montagne f mountain
montant m amount
monter get on, go up
monter à cheval ride (vb)
montre f watch (n)
montrer show (vb)
monument m monument
morceau m slice (n)
mordre bite (vb)
morsure f bite (n, animal)

mort f death
mort(e) dead
morue f cod
mosquée f mosque
mot m word
moteur m motor, engine
motif m pattern
moto f motorbike
mots croisés m crossword puzzle
mouche f fly (n)
mouchoir m handkerchief
mouchoir en papier m tissue
mouette f seagull
mouillage m mooring
mouillé(e) wet
moules fpl mussels
mourir die (vb)
moustache f moustache
moustique m mosquito
moutarde f mustard
mouton m mutton, sheep
moyen m medium
moyen(ne) average
mur m wall
mûr(e) ripe
muscle m muscle
musée m museum
musicien/musicienne musician
Musulman(e) Muslim
myope short-sighted

FRENCH → ENGLISH

N

n'importe qui anybody
n'importe quoi
  anything
nager swim
naissance f birth
nappe f tablecloth
national(e) national
nationalité f nationality
natte f plait
nature f nature
naturel/naturelle
  natural
nausée f nausea
navigation de plaisir f
  sailing
navire m ship
né(e) born
ne ... pas not
nécessaire necessary
négatif/négative
  negative
neige f snow
néo-zélandais(e),
  Néo-Zélandais (e)
  New Zealander
neuf/neuve new
  (brand)
neveu m nephew
nez m nose
ni ... ni neither ... nor
nid m nest
nièce f niece
Noël m Christmas
nœud papillon m bow
  tie
noir(e) black
noisette f hazelnut

noix f nut, walnut
noix de coco f
  coconut
nom m name, surname
nom de jeune fille m
  maiden name
nombre m number
non no
non-fumeurs non-
  smoking
non-sucré(e) savoury,
  unsweetened
nord m north
Norvège f Norway
norvégien(ne),
  Norvégien(ne)
  Norwegian
nos our
nostalgie f
  homesickness
note f note (n)
noter note (vb)
notre our
nounou f nanny
nourrir feed
nourriture f food
nous us, we
nous sommes we are
nouveau/nouvelle
  new
Nouvel An m New Year
Nouvelle-Zélande f
  New Zealand
nouvelles f news
novembre November
nuage m cloud
nuit f night

numéro d'immatriculation m
number plate, registration number

numéro de téléphone m
phone number

nursery f nursery

O

objets de valeur mpl
valuables (n)

objets trouvés mpl
lost property

obligatoire compulsory

obsèques f funeral

obtenir get, obtain

occupation f
occupation

occupé(e) busy, engaged, occupied

océan m ocean

Océan Atlantique m
Atlantic Ocean

octobre October

odeur f smell (n)

œil eye

œuf m egg

œufs brouillés m
scrambled eggs

oie f goose

oignon m onion

oiseau m bird

olive f olive

ombre f shade

ombre à paupières f
eye shadow

ombrelle f sunshade

omelette f omelette

oncle m uncle

ongle m nail

opéra m opera

opérateur/opératrice
operator (phone)

opération f operation

opération chirurgicale f
surgery (procedure)

opticien/opticienne
optician

or m gold

orage m thunderstorm

orange f orange

orchestre m orchestra, stalls

ordinateur m computer

ordonnance f
prescription

ordures f litter (n), rubbish, trash

oreille f ear

oreiller m pillow

oreillons mpl mumps

orteil m toe

os m bone

otite f earache

ou or

où? where?

ou ... ou either ... or

oublier forget

ouest m west

oui yes

ourlet m hem

outil m tool

ouvert(e) open (adj)

FRENCH → ENGLISH

ouvre-boîte m can opener, tin opener
ouvrir open (vb), unlock

P
pacemaker m pacemaker
page f page
Pages Jaunes fpl Yellow Pages
paille f straw
pain m bread, loaf
pain complet wholemeal bread
pain de seigle m rye bread
paire f pair
palace m palace, hotel
palais m palace
pâle pale
palmes f flippers
panier m basket
panne f breakdown
panne d'électricité f power cut
panneau d'affichage m notice board
panneau indicateur m road sign
pantalon m trousers, pants
pantoufles f slippers
papeterie f stationer's
papier m paper
papier cadeau m wrapping paper

papier d'aluminium m tinfoil
papier d'emballage m wrapping paper
papillon m butterfly
Pâques Easter
paquet m package
par by, per, through
par exemple for example
par ici over here
par là over there, this way
parapluie m umbrella
parasol m sunshade
parc m park
parce que because
parcmètre m parking meter
pardessus m overcoat
pardon? pardon? what?
pardon! sorry!
pare-brise m windscreen
pare-choc m bumper
pare-feu m fender
parent m relative, relation
parents m parents
paresseux/ paresseuse lazy
parfait! fine!
parfait(e) perfect
parfois occasionally
parfum m perfume, scent, flavour
pari m bet (n)

parier bet (vb)
parler talk (vb)
parmi among
partager share (vb)
partenaire m/f partner (game)
parti m party (political)
parti(e) away
partie f part
partir leave (vb), depart, go away
partout everywhere
pas m step (n)
pas cher cheap
pas frais stale
passage m footpath
passage à niveau m level crossing
passage pour piétons m pedestrian crossing
passager/passagère passenger
passé(e) past
passeport m passport
passer pass (vb)
passer la nuit overnight (to stay)
passionnant(e) exciting
passoire f colander, sieve
pastèque f watermelon
pastilles pour la gorge fpl throat lozenges
pâté de foie liver pâté
patient(e) patient
patin m skate (n)

patinoire f ice rink, skating rink
patins à glace m ice skates
pâtisserie f cake shop, pastry
pause f break (n)
pauvre poor
payé(e) paid
payer trop cher overcharge (vb)
pays m country, land
Pays-Bas mpl Netherlands
Pays de Galles m Wales
paysage m scenery
PCV reverse charge call
péage m toll
peau f skin
pêche f peach
pédale f pedal
peigne m comb
peindre paint (vb)
peinture f painting
peler peel (vb)
pelle f dustpan
pendant during
pendant que while
penderie f wardrobe
péninsule f peninsula
penser think
pension f boarding house, guesthouse
pension complète f full board
pépinière f nursery (plants)

perceuse f drill (n)
perdre lose
perdu(e) lost
père m father
performance f
performance
période f period (time)
périphérique m ring
road
perle f pearl
permanente f perm
permettre allow
permis m licence,
permit
permis de chasse m
hunting permit
permis de conduire m
driving licence
permis de pêche m
fishing permit
perruque f wig
personne f nobody,
person
personne âgée senior
citizen
peser weigh
pétillant(e) sparkling,
fizzy
petit(e) little, short, small
petit déjeuner m
breakfast
petit pain m roll (food)
petit pois mpl peas
petit-fils m grandson
petite-fille f granddaughter
pétrole m petrol
peu few, little

peu profond(e)
shallow
peuple m people
peut-être maybe,
perhaps
phares m headlights
pharmacie f pharmacy
pharmacien(ne)
chemist
photo f photo
photocopie f
photocopy
phrase f sentence
piano m piano
pic m peak
pichet m jug
pickpocket m
pickpocket
pièce f coin, piece,
room
pièce (theatre) f
play (n)
pièce de rechange f
spare part
pied m foot
pieds m feet
pierre f stone
piéton m pedestrian
pilote m pilot
pilule f pill
pince à épiler f
tweezers
pince à linge f clothes
peg
pinceau m brush
pinces fpl pliers
pipe f pipe
pique-nique m picnic

piquer sting (vb)
piquet (de tente) m tent peg
piqûre f injection, sting (n)
piqûre d'insecte f insect bite
pire worse
piscine couverte f indoor pool
piste cyclable f cycle track
piste (de ski) f ski slope
piste pour débutants f nursery slope
pitié f pity (n)
placard m cupboard
place f place, room, seat, square (n)
place côté fenêtre f window seat
plafond m ceiling
plage f beach
plage de nudistes f nudist beach
plainte f complaint
plaisanter joke (vb)
plan m map
plan des rues m street map
planche à repasser f ironing board
planche de surf f surfboard
plante f plant
plaque minéralogique f number plate

plastique m plastic
plat(e) flat (adj)
plat m course (meals)
plat principal m main course
plateau m tray
plate-forme f platform
platine laser f CD player
plâtre m plaster (building)
plats à emporter mpl takeaway food
plein(e) full
plein(e) de monde crowded
plein tarif m peak rate
pleurer cry (vb)
plier bend (vb)
plomb m lead (n)
plombage m filling (tooth)
plombier m plumber
plongée sous-marine f scuba diving
pluie f rain
plumeau m duster
plus more
plus loin further
plus ou moins about, approximately
plus tard later
plusieurs several
pneu m tyre
pneu à plat flat tyre
pneu de secour m spare tyre
poche f pocket

FRENCH → ENGLISH

poché(e) poached

poêle f frying pan

poids m weight

poignée f handle

point m stitch
(n, sewing)

point de suture m
stitch (n, medical)

pointe f point (n)

points m points

pointu(e) sharp

pointure f size (shoes)

poire f pear

poireau m leek

poison m poison

poisson m fish

poissonnier m
fishmonger

poitrine f breast, chest

poivre m pepper (spice)

poivron m pepper
(vegetable)

poli(e) polite

police f police

policier m policeman

polir polish (vb)

pollué(e) polluted

Pologne f Poland

polonais(e) Polish

Polonais(e) Pole

pommade f ointment

pomme de terre f
potato

pompe f pump (n)

pomper pump (vb)

pompiers mpl fire
brigade

pont bridge

pontage m bypass
(medical)

populaire popular

population f population

porc m pork

porcelaine f china

port m harbour, port

porte f gate

porte-bagages m
luggage rack

porte-clé m key ring

porte-documents m
briefcase

porte-feuille m wallet

porte-manteau m
hanger, coat hanger

porte-monnaie m
purse

porter carry, wear

porteur m porter

portion f portion

porto m port (wine)

portrait m portrait

**portugais(e),
Portugais(e)**
Portuguese

Portugal m Portugal

pose f exposure (photo)

**pose d'une prothèse
de la hanche** f hip
replacement

possible possible

poste m post

Poste f postal service

poste centrale f main
post office

poster m poster

pot d'échappement m
exhaust pipe
poteau indicateur m
signpost
poterie f pottery
poubelle f bin, dustbin,
waste bin
pouce m inch, thumb
poudre f powder
poudre à laver f soap
powder
poulet m chicken
pour for
pourboire m tip (n)
pourquoi? why?
pourri(e) rotten
pousser push
poussette f pushchair
poussière f dust (n)
pouvoir can, be able to,
may, might
pratique f practice
pratiquer practise
préféré(e) favourite
préférer prefer
premier/première first
premier étage m
first floor
premier ministre m
prime minister
première classe f
first class
premièrement at first
prendre take
**prendre du bon
temps** enjoy
prendre l'avion
fly (vb, plane)

prendre une photo
take a photo
prénom m Christian
name, first name
près near
présent(e) present (adj)
présenter present (vb)
préservatif m
condom
presque almost
pressing m dry
cleaner's
pression f pressure
pression des pneus f
tyre pressure
prêt(e) ready
prêter lend
prêtre m priest
**prévision
météorologique** f
weather forecast
prier pray
principal(e) main
printemps m spring
prise f plug (electric)
prise de courant
socket (electric)
prison f prison
privé(e) private
prix m price, prize,
charge, cost
probablement
probably
problème m problem
proche near
produit insectifuge m
insect repellent

FRENCH → ENGLISH

FRENCH → ENGLISH

produit pour la vaisselle m
washing-up liquid

professeur m/f
teacher

profond(e) deep

programme m
programme, program

promenade f ride (n),
walk (n)

promesse f
promise (n)

promettre promise (vb)

prononcer pronounce

propre clean

propriétaire m/f owner,
landlord, landlady,

prospectus m leaflet

protestant(e)
Protestant

prudent(e) careful

prune f plum

public m audience

public/publique
public

publicité f
advertisement

puce f flea

pull m jumper, pullover,
_sweater

pull-over m pullover

purée de pommes de terre f mashed
potatoes

pyjama m pyjamas

Pyrénées fpl
Pyrenees

Q

quai m quay

qualité f quality

quand? when?

quantité f quantity

quarantaine f
quarantine

quart m quarter
(fraction)

quartier m quarter
(part of town)

Quartier Latin m Latin
Quarter

quatre-quatre f four-
wheel drive

que that

qu'est-ce qui ne va pas? what is wrong?

qu'est-ce qu'il y a?
what's the matter?

quel/quelle? which?

quelle heure est-il?
what time is it?

quelque chose
something

quelque part
somewhere

quelques a few, couple,
some

quelqu'un somebody,
someone

question f question

queue f queue (n)

qui that

qui? who?

quincaillerie m
hardware shop

quincaillerie f
ironmonger's
quinzaine de jours f
fortnight
quitter leave (vb)
quotidien(ne) daily

R

raccourci m short cut
raccrocher hang up
(telephone)
race f race
radiateur m radiator
radio f radio
radiographie f X-ray
radis m radish
rage f rabies
ragoût m stew
raide steep
raisin m grapes
raisin sec m raisin
raisonnable reasonable
rame f oar
rangée f row (n)
râpé(e) grated
rapide fast
rapport m connection,
report (n)
rapporter report (vb)
raquette f racket
raquette de tennis f
tennis racket
rare rare (seldom)
raser shave
rasoir m razor
rassis stale
rat m rat
râteau m rake

rayon m department
(in a store), spoke
(n, of wheel)
rayon de soleil m
sunshine
rayons X mpl X-ray
récemment recently
réception f reception
réceptionniste m/f
receptionist
recette f recipe
receveur m receiver
recharger recharge
recommander
recommend
réconfortant
cheering
reconnaissant(e)
grateful
reconnaître
recognize
reçu m receipt
recueillir collect (vb)
reculer reverse
réduction f reduction
réduire reduce
réel/réelle real
réfrigérateur m fridge
refuser refuse (vb)
regarder look at
régime m diet
région f region
registre m register (n)
règle f ruler
règles fpl period
(physiology)
rein m kidney (organ)
reine f queen

FRENCH → ENGLISH

FRENCH → ENGLISH

rembourser refund (vb)
remercier thank
remorque f trailer
remorquer tow
remplir fill
remplissez fill in
renard m fox
rencontre f meeting
rencontrer meet
rendez-vous m
 appointment
rendre give back
renseignement m
 information
renverser knock over,
 spill (vb)
renvoyer à plus tard
 postpone
réparer fix (vb), mend,
 repair
repas m meal
répéter repeat
répondre answer (vb),
 reply (vb)
repos m rest
 (relaxation)
représentant(e) de
 commerce sales
 representative
représentation f
 performance (theatre)
République Tchèque f
 Czech Republic
réservation f
 reservation
réserve f reserve (n),
 stock

réserve naturelle f
 nature reserve
réserver book (vb),
 reserve (vb)
réservoir m tank
résident(e) resident
respirer breathe
reste m rest (remainder)
rester remain, stay
retiré(e) secluded
retour m return (n)
retraité(e) retired (adj),
 old-age pensioner
rétrécir shrink (vb)
rétroviseur m rearview
 mirror
retourner go back
réunion f meeting
réveil m clock
réveil téléphonique m
 wake-up call
réveillé(e) awake
Réveillon de Noël m
 Christmas Eve
revenir come back,
 return (vb)
révoltant(e) revolting
rez-de-chaussée m
 ground floor
Rhin m Rhine
rhum m rum
rhumatisme m
 rheumatism
rhume des foins m
 hay fever
riche rich
rideau m curtain

ridicule ridiculous
rien nothing
rien d'autre nothing else
rire laugh (vb)
rivage m shore
rivière f river
riz m rice
robe f dress (n)
robe de chambre f dressing gown
roc m rock (n)
rocher m rock (n)
rognon m kidney (food)
roi m king
roman m novel
rond(e) round
ronfler snore
rose pink
rose f rose
roue f wheel
roue de secour f spare wheel
rouge red
rouge à lèvres m lipstick
rougeole f measles
rouillé(e) rusty
rouleau m coil (n), roll (n)
rouler roll (vb)
route f road
route à péage f toll road
royal(e) royal
Royaume-Uni m U.K.
ruban m ribbon

ruban adhésif m adhesive tape
rubéole f German measles, rubella
rue f street
rue à sens unique f one-way street
rue principale f main road
rugueux/rugueuse rough (surface)
ruine f ruin
ruisseau m stream

S
s'allonger lie down
s'amuser enjoy
s'arrêter stop (vb)
s'asseoir sit
s'attendre à expect
sa his, her (possessive)
sable m sand
sabot m wheel clamp
sac m bag
sac à dos m backpack
sac à main m handbag
sac de couchage m sleeping bag
sac (en plastique) m carrier bag
sac isotherme m cool bag/box
sachet de thé m tea bag
saignant(e) rare (meat), underdone

saigner bleed
sain(e) healthy
saint(e) holy
Saint-Sylvestre f New Year's Eve
saison f season
salade f salad
salaire m wage
sale dirty
salé(e) savoury
salle f ward (hospital)
salle à manger f dining room
salle d'attente f waiting room
salle d'embarquement f departure lounge
salle de bains f bathroom
salon m lounge
salon d'essayage m fitting room
salutations fpl greeting
samedi m Saturday
sandales fpl sandals
sandales de plage f flip flops
sandwich m sandwich
sang m blood
sanglier m boar
sans without
sans alcool non-alcoholic
sans connaissance unconscious
sans danger safe (adj)

sans façon informal
sans plomb lead-free
sans sucre sugar-free
satisfait(e) pleased
sauce f sauce
saucisse f sausage
sauf except
saumon m salmon
saumon fumé m smoked salmon
sauter jump (vb)
sauvetage en montagne m mountain rescue
savoir know (something)
savon m soap
s'échapper escape (vb)
s'effondrer collapse (vb)
s'évanouir faint(vb)
se battre fight (vb)
se gratter scratch (vb)
se laver wash
se lever get up
se passer happen
se plaindre complain
se précipiter rush (vb)
se rappeler remember
se réjouir à l'idée de look forward to
se rendre compte realize
se reposer rest (vb)
se retourner turn around

se réveiller wake up

se souvenir remember

seau m bucket, pail

sec dry

sèche dry

séchoir m dryer

séchoir à cheveux m hairdryer

second(e) second

secouer shake

secourir rescue (vb)

secours m rescue (n)

secours d'urgence m first aid

secrétaire m/f secretary

sein m breast

seins nus topless

séjour m living room

sel m salt

selle f saddle

semelle f sole (shoe)

sensationnel amazing

sentence f sentence

sentier m footpath, path

sentir feel, smell (vb)

séparer separate (vb)

septembre September

septique septic

sérieux/sérieuse serious

serpent m snake

serpillière f floorcloth

serré(e) tight

serrure f lock (n)

serveur/serveuse waiter/waitress

service m department, service (n), service charge

service des urgences m casualty/emergency department

serviette (de table) napkin

serviette de toilette f towel

serviette en papier f paper napkin

serviettes hygiéniques fpl sanitary pads

seul(e) alone, single

seulement only

sexe m sex

shampooing et mise en plis m shampoo and set

short m shorts

s'il vous plaît please

s'inscrire à join (club), register (vb)

si if, yes

siècle m century

siège m seat

siège auto pour enfants m child car seat

signal m signal

signature f signature

signe m sign (n)

signer sign (vb)

FRENCH → ENGLISH

signifier mean (vb)
silence m silence
similaire similar
simple informal, plain, simple
sirop pour la toux m cough mixture
ski m ski (n)
ski nautique m water skiing
skier ski (vb)
slip m knickers, panties, underpants
slovaque, Slovaque Slovak
Slovaquie f Slovak Republic
s'occuper de look after
sobre sober
socquettes f socks
soda m soda
sœur f sister
soie f silk
soigner look after, care (for)
soir m evening
soirée f evening, party (celebration)
soit ... soit either ... or
sol m floor, ground
soldes m sale
sole f sole (fish)
soleil m sun
solide tough
soluble soluble
sombre dark
somme due f due

sommet m summit, top
somnifère m sleeping pill
son his, her (possessive)
sonner ring (vb)
sonnette f bell
sorte f sort
sorti(e) out
sortie f exit
sortie de secours f emergency exit, fire exit
soucoupe f saucer
soudain suddenly
souhaiter wish (vb)
soûl(e) drunk
soulever lift (vb)
soupape f valve
soupe f soup
source chaude f hot spring
sourd(e) deaf
sourire m smile (n)
sourire smile (vb)
souris f mouse
sous under
sous-sol m basement
sous-titre m subtitle
sous-vêtement m underwear
soutien-gorge m bra
souvenir m souvenir
souvent often
sparadrap m sticking plaster
spécialement especially
spécialité f speciality

spectacle m show (n)

spectacle de marionnettes m puppet show

stade m stadium

star f star (film)

starter m starter (car)

station de taxis taxi rank

station de vacances f resort

station-service f petrol station

station thermale f spa

statue f statue

stimulateur cardiaque m pacemaker

stop m stop (n)

store m blind (n)

stupéfiant amazing

stupide stupid

stylo m pen

stylo bille m ballpoint pen

sucette f lollipop

sucre m sugar

sucré(e) sweet (adj)

sud m south

sud-africain(e), Sud-Africain(e) South African

Suède f Sweden

suédois(e), Suédois(e) Swedish

sueur f sweat (n)

suis am

Suisse f Switzerland

suisse, Suisse/Suissesse Swiss

suivant(e) next

suivre follow

supplément m supplement

supplémentaire extra

sur on

sûr(e) safe (adj), sure

surchauffer overheat

surgelé(e) frozen (food)

surtout mostly

survêtement m tracksuit

suspension f suspension

suturer stitch (vb, medical)

synagogue f synagogue

synthétique m man-made fibre

T

ta your

table f table

tablette de chocolat f bar of chocolate

tablier m apron

tache f stain (n)

taie d'oreiller f pillowcase

taille f size (clothing), waist

tailleur m tailor, suit (woman)

FRENCH → ENGLISH

FRENCH → ENGLISH

talc m talcum powder
talon m heel
tamis de cuisine m sieve
tampon m tampon
tante f aunt
tapis m carpet
tard late
tarif m fare
tarif étudiant m student discount
tarif postal m postage
tasse f cup
taux (de change) m rate (of exchange)
taxe f tax
taxi m taxi, cab
teinture f dye (n)
teinturier m dry cleaner's
télécarte f phone card
télécopie f fax
téléphérique m cable car
téléphone m telephone
téléphone mobile m mobile phone
téléphone public m payphone
télésiège m chair lift
télévision f television
témoin m witness (n)
température f temperature, fever
tempête f storm
temple m temple
temporaire temporary

temps m time, weather
tendon m tendon
tenir hold (vb)
tennis m tennis
tension artérielle f blood pressure
tente f tent
terminal(e) terminal (adj)
terminé(e) over
terminus m terminal (n)
terne dull
terrain de camping m camp site
terrain de golf golf course
terre f earth, land
terrible awful, dreadful
tes your
tête f head
tétine f teat (bottle)
thé m tea
théâtre m theatre
théière f teapot
thermomètre f thermometer
thermos f flask
thon m tuna
ticket m ticket
timbre m stamp
timbre-poste m postage stamp
timide shy
tire-bouchon m corkscrew
tirer pull
tiroir m drawer

tisane f herbal tea
tissu m material
titre de transport m travel document
toile f web
toilettes f lavatory, toilet
toit m roof
toit ouvrant m sunroof
tomate f tomato
tomber drop, fall (vb)
ton your
tonalité f dialling tone
tongs f flip flops
tonneau m barrel
tonnerre m thunder
torche électrique f flashlight
total m total (n)
total(e) total (adj)
toujours always, still
tour f tower
tour m tour
tour-opérateur m tour operator
tourner turn
tournevis m screwdriver
tourte f pie
tous les deux both
tous les jours daily
tousser cough (vb)
tout everything
tout/toute whole
tout à fait altogether, quite

tout de suite straightaway
tout droit straight on
tout près nearby
toutes les heures hourly
toux f cough (n)
toxique poisonous
traducteur/ traductrice translator
traduction f translation
traduire translate
train m train
traîneau m sledge
tram m tram
tramway m tram
tranchant(e) sharp
tranche f slice (n)
tranquille quiet
tranquillisant m tranquiliser
transpirer sweat (vb)
travail m job, work (n)
travailler work (vb)
travaux m road works
traveller's chèque m traveller's cheque
traverser cross (vb)
tremblement de terre m earthquake
tremplin (de ski) m ski jump
très very
tresse f plait
tricot de corps m vest

FRENCH → ENGLISH

tricoter knit
triste sad
trop cuit overdone (food)
trottoir m pavement, sidewalk
trou m hole
trouble m trouble
trousse à outils f tool kit
trousse à pharmacie f first-aid kit
trouver find (vb)
truite f trout
tu you
tuba m snorkel (n)
tuer kill (vb)
tunnel m tunnel
turc/turque Turkish
Turc/Turque Turk
Turquie f Turkey
turquoise f turquoise
tuyau d'arrosage m hose pipe
TVA f VAT
type m type
typique typical

U

ulcère m ulcer
un(e) one, a, an
un(e) autre another
une fois once
université f university
urgence f emergency
urgent(e) urgent
usine f factory

ustensiles de cuisine mpl cooking ustensils
utile useful
utiliser use (vb)

V

vacance f vacancy
vacances fpl holiday, vacation
vaccin m vaccination
vache f cow
vague f wave (n)
vaisselle f crockery
valeur f value (n), worth (n)
valide valid
valise f suitcase
vallée f valley
vanille f vanilla
vapeur f steam
varicelle f chicken pox
veau m calf (animal), veal
vedette star (sky)
végétarien(ne) vegetarian
véhicule m vehicle
veine f vein
vélo m bicycle
vendeur/vendeuse salesperson, shop assistant
vendre sell
vendredi m Friday
Vendredi Saint m Good Friday

vénéneux/vénéneuse poisonous

venir come

vent m wind

vente f sale

ventilateur m fan (n)

ver m maggot

verglas m black ice

vérifier check (vb)

vernis à ongles m nail varnish/polish

verre m glass, lens

verres de contact m contact lenses

verser pour

vert(e) green

veste f jacket

vestiaire m changing room, cloakroom

vêtements mpl clothes

vêtements pour femmes mpl ladies' wear

vêtements pour hommes mpl menswear

vétérinaire m/f vet, veterinarian

veuve/veuf widow/er

via via

viande f meat

viande hachée f minced meat

vide empty

vie f life

vieux/vieille old

vignoble m vineyard

village m village

ville f town

vin m wine

vin de table m table wine

vin rouge m red wine

vinaigre m vinegar

vinaigrette f salad dressing

viol m rape

violet/violette purple

violette f violet

virage m bend (n)

virus m virus

vis f screw

visa m visa

visage m face

visite f visit (n)

visiter visit (vb)

vite quickly

vitesse f speed

vitrine f shop window

vivant(e) lively

vivre live (vb)

vœu m wish (n)

voilier m yacht

vol m theft

volé(e) stolen

voler fly (vb, bird)

voleur/voleuse thief

voile f sail

voir see

voisin/voisine neighbour

voiture f car

voiture-buffet f buffet car

FRENCH → ENGLISH

voiture d'enfant f
  pram
voiture de location f
  hire car
voix f voice
vol m flight
volant m steering
  wheel
volcan m volcano
voler steal
volet m shutter
voltage m voltage
vomir vomit (vb)
vos your
votre your
vouloir want
vous you
vous êtes you are
voyage m journey
voyage d'affaires m
  business trip
voyage organisé m
  guided tour, package
  holiday
voyager travel (vb)
vrai(e) real, true
vraiment really
vue f sight, view

W
wagon m carriage
wagon-lit m sleeper,
  sleeping car
web m web
week-end m
  weekend

Y
yacht m yacht
yeux m eyes
youyou m dinghy

Z
zéro m zero
zona m shingles
zone f area, zone
zoo m zoo